GET A
LITERARY
AGENT

WRITER'S DIGEST
BOOKS

WritersDigest.*com*
Cincinnati, Ohio

GET A
LITERARY
AGENT

The Complete Guide to Securing
Representation for Your Work

CHUCK SAMBUCHINO

For more resources for writers, visit www.writersdigest.com.

19 18 17 16 15 5 4 3 2 1

Distributed in Canada by Fraser Direct
100 Armstrong Avenue
Georgetown, Ontario, Canada L7G 5S4
Tel: (905) 877-4411

Distributed in the U.K. and Europe by F&W Media International
Brunel House, Newton Abbot, Devon, TQ12 4PU, England
Tel: (+44) 1626-323200, Fax: (+44) 1626-323319
E-mail: postmaster@davidandcharles.co.uk

Distributed in Australia by Capricorn Link
P.O. Box 704, Windsor, NSW 2756 Australia
Tel: (02) 4577-3555

Edited by **Melissa Wuske and Rachel Randall**
Designed by **Bethany Rainbolt**
Production coordinated by **Debbie Thomas**

Dedication

For Bre

Acknowledgments

As usual, I want to thank the women who made this book possible. The first is my wife, Bre, for all her love and support. The second is my young daughter, Geneva, for just being overwhelmingly cute and adorable. The third is my agent, Sorche Fairbank, for her constant efforts as an advocate. Special thanks also goes out to Phil Sexton, publisher of Writer's Digest Books, for his stewardship and guidance.

And I am well aware that this book would not be possible without the input and feedback of so many literary agents who gave quotes and material to fill these pages. More than one hundred agents offered guidance in this book, and I thank every one of them. They're on the front lines and deserve credit for all the wisdom they shared in this book.

Lastly, I want to thank my awesome beta readers, including agents Karen Grencik, Carlie Webber, and Kimiko Nakamura.

About the Author

Chuck Sambuchino (@chucksambuchino) of Writer's Digest Books edits the *Guide to Literary Agents* and the *Children's Writer's & Illustrator's Market*. His *Guide to Literary Agents* blog is one of the largest blogs in publishing. His 2010 humor book, *How to Survive a Garden Gnome Attack*, was optioned by Sony Pictures. His books have been mentioned in *Reader's Digest*, *USA Today*, *The New York Times*, *The Huffington Post*, *Variety*, and more. Chuck has also authored the writing guides *Formatting & Submitting Your Manuscript* (2009) and *Create Your Writer Platform* (2012). Besides that, he is a husband, a sleep-deprived new father, and the owner of a flabby dog named Graham.

TABLE OF CONTENTS

Part Three: Giving Yourself the Best Chance Possible

Appendix: Glossary and Resources

INTRODUCTION

When I joined Writer's Digest a decade ago and began to meet aspiring authors in person, many would walk up to me and ask the same question: "How do I get a literary agent?" Ten years later, as I shake hands with new writers at conferences, I still get asked the same question.

Getting an agent to sign you and sell your books is a challenging task. Who are the best ones to contact? What are the ins and outs and best practices for querying agents? How do you give your book the best chance of being read and considered?

These types of questions are the reason I wrote this book. I wanted to give writers a comprehensive resource to address the many frequently asked questions that arise during the journey to find a literary agent. The goal was to create a guide that would offer the advice of numerous knowledgeable agents as well as provide examples of submission materials that speak to *all* book writers, regardless of category or genre.

The Internet is, unfortunately, a breeding ground for misinformation and half-truths on any subject—including how to query and sign with an agent. Many frustrated writers say that an agent won't represent you before you've had a book published, but you can't sell a book without an agent—thus creating a catch-22. It's just not true—and it's exactly the type of myth I want to dispel so writers can give themselves the best chance going forward.

In fact, having the best chance at writing and publishing success all comes down to *educating yourself*—about the craft of writing, professionalism and submissions, research and targeting, genres and book categories, individual agents and their quirks, and so on. The more you learn, the better your chances of finding an agent and publishing a book.

So, without further ado, let's help you find a literary agent as soon as possible.

PART ONE

GETTING READY TO PITCH

CHAPTER ONE

THE SKINNY ON AGENTS

(AND WHY YOU WANT ONE)

If you're reading this, chances are you've either written a book or are in the middle of writing one. And chances are, at some point, you've heard a friend or peer explain that you should get a literary agent. But let's slow down for a moment. What is an agent? What does she do? What role does she play in your career? What value does she bring to the table? (Approximately 85 percent of agents are women, so I'll use the pronoun *she* in this book. But male agents certainly do exist and perform very well at their jobs.)

In short, a literary agent represents you in an effort to sell your book-length works to publishers. She serves as a conduit for getting your work to specific editors who are interested in buying the types of books you write. In other words, the agent's foremost responsibility is to get your work into the hands of the specific decision-making persons who can acquire the project and enact a deal for money. Agents are *connectors*—bridging the wide chasm between writers and editors in an effort to bring books to life.

Besides having the ability to sell books, agents also protect your interests, guide your career, and handle many of the business responsibilities that go along with selling manuscripts. For her efforts, your agent gets a small percentage of all monies you make off a project.

"Your agent is not your shrink or your mother or your administrative assistant. Your agent is your friendly publishing professional dedicated to selling your work and building your career. Remember that when the rejections start coming in—and the checks, too!"

—Paula Munier (Talcott Notch Literary Services)

DO YOU NEED AN AGENT?

At one point or another, you've probably asked yourself the following questions: *Do I really need an agent? Can I just go it alone and keep the entire payment for my book?* The answers depend on the type of book you're writing or have written.

If you're writing nonfiction, the decision to get an agent should rest on whether your book has any *limitations*. Perhaps you're writing a book about present-day Native American culture in Oklahoma. Such a book has limitations. It's about a niche topic (Native American culture), and it also has a regional focus (in this case, Oklahoma). It could very well be a masterful book, but because of these two distinct limitations, the title will likely sell fewer than 7,500 copies. The book is small in both scope and sales potential. This is exactly the type of nonfiction book you *don't* need an agent for. Skip the agent, and go straight to an academic or small publisher for a deal. In fact, even if you wanted agent representation, it's not likely that an agent would actually sign you, because her financial compensation would be so meager. If a small publisher offers you $1,500 up front for the book, the agent's share (at 15 percent) is $225. That isn't a big incentive for her to get involved.

On the flip side, if you're writing a nonfiction book that has *no* significant limitations, then I believe you should seek an agent who can get you the best deal with a quality publisher. Plenty of books have mainstream, commercial appeal with the potential to reach many different audiences. Examples of this could be anything from cookbooks, memoir, and how-to titles to a diet book called *How to Lose 10 Pounds in 10 Weeks*. Other books are niche titles and have smaller, more focused target audiences—such as a guidebook on the best restaurants in San Francisco.

This same line of thinking goes for novels. If you're writing a book that's incredibly niche—say, a *science fiction–erotica hybrid*—then you can likely approach a publisher on your own for a small, solid deal. But if the book has any kind of mainstream potential, it's best to look for an agent.

WHY DO YOU NEED AN AGENT?

To answer this, I turn to literary agent Mollie Glick of Foundry Literary + Media. She addressed this question at a writers conference once and explained that, while agents can bring many elements to a writer-agent relationship—such as hands-on editing and career guidance—their true value is in the three key things they bring to the table that writers can rarely do themselves.

1. **AN AGENT DEVELOPS CLOSE RELATIONSHIPS WITH EDITORS AND KNOWS THE BEST POTENTIAL PUBLISHERS FOR YOUR WORK.** An agent's primary job is to know which editors at which publishing houses are seeking which categories of material. Not only will a good agent know that XYZ Editor acquires literary fiction, but she'll know that XYZ Editor is currently calling for literary fiction set in Asia with a female protagonist. A good agent is aware of these little-known "likes" and is sensitive to trend changes that affect editor preferences on a month-by-month basis. This is important because publishing is a very relationship-based industry.

An agent will follow the tastes and wants of editors all over the country. She does this so that when an excellent manuscript lands on her desk, she knows precisely where to send it. An agent won't simply search online for "publishing houses seeking mystery novels" like a writer would. She already knows which editors are seeking mysteries and at what imprints.

These relationships are so valuable because many of the editors at large houses are closed to unsolicited submissions from writers—meaning they do not invite amateur writers they don't know to contact them directly. If you want to pitch editors at Penguin Random House or Knopf, your work must be submitted through an agent. Editors count on agents to act as gatekeepers who sift through the slush piles to find the gems that truly deserve consideration for publication. All editors I know are drastically overworked and need help filtering through the majority of inappropriate submissions to focus on the best targeted and most promising. This is where agents come in—*they get your book read.*

Without an agent, a writer can pitch directly to a small publishing house and, often, a midsize house. But can this same writer pitch to Candlewick or HarperCollins or Simon & Schuster? No. If you skip the agent, you close yourself off to most of the biggest potential markets. And if you do pitch to a midsize publishing house that takes queries directly from writers, no doubt your submission would get more attention if it came from an agent. Agented novels and proposals carry the weight of having already been vetted and polished by a trustworthy professional.

2. **AN AGENT IS VERY FAMILIAR WITH PUBLISHING CONTRACTS AND FIGHTS TO GET YOU THE BEST DEAL POSSIBLE.** Here's some bad news: Publishing house contracts are not written with the writer's benefit in mind. The first offer you see will not be im-

pressive. That's just the nature of the beast; it's a process of negotiation. You'll seek a lot, they'll offer a little, and a good agent will help both parties meet in the middle.

An agent reviews and negotiates contracts every week. She's familiar with legal jargon and boilerplate deals, and with which royalty structures will get you the most money. In fact, every line of a contract is a concern to her. If a contractual clause is bad, she fights to make it okay. If it's okay, she fights to make it good. If it's good, she fights to make it great. A capable agent will fight on nearly every point—because it's in both of your best interests. The more she fights, the more her client (i.e., you) makes. And the more her client makes, the greater the sum she earns off her 15 percent commission.

No one is more familiar with book contracts than an agent, and no one will battle harder for you. On a related note, your agent is the one who will notify the publisher's accounting department if your payment is late and have them process the check. She's the one who makes sure that your foreign rights and excerpt payments are issued, for instance.

3. **AN AGENT CAN SERVE AS A BUFFER BETWEEN YOU AND YOUR EDITOR—ACTING AS A "BAD COP" WHEN THE NEED ARISES.** Let's say your editor sends you the first version of your book's cover design and explains how much everyone at the publishing house loves it. But here's the problem: You think it stinks to high heaven. If you tell the editor as much, even in a nice way, the situation can become awkward. So what's a writer to do? Use bad-cop agent, that's what.

An editor can get mad at your agent, but he should never be mad at you. Because your editor is the foremost champion of your book to other personnel at the publishing house, it's imperative that your relationship with him remains positive.

"Publishing is a business, but writing is an art form. An agent can take care of the business aspects of a writer's career and allow them to write, which is probably what authors want to be doing more of anyway."

—Suzie Townsend (New Leaf Literary and Media)

Most of us have lofty expectations for our work, whether we verbalize them aloud or not. When we dream of publishing books, we likely dream of the following.

- Having our books distributed to all major bookstores nationwide
- Receiving a sizable up-front advance payment (i.e., more money) that is ours to keep and making sure we get fair royalties
- Seeing our books in Hudson Booksellers and all other airport stores
- Selling foreign-language rights to overseas territories so that our stories can be enjoyed in other countries and we can, in turn, get paid more
- Negotiating film deals with Hollywood for a chance to see our books become movies and, again, generate revenue
- Receiving publicity and marketing assistance from an individual (or several) at the publishing house, whose job is to increase book sales
- Retiring from our day jobs!

These are the things I dream of—as I expect you do, too. So how do you accomplish these goals? From everything I've seen, the best way is to sign with a large publishing house that has the staff, money, contacts, and infrastructure to make it happen. And how does one sell to a large publishing house? Only with agent representation to bridge the gap.

That, in my opinion, is why you need an agent. Sure, an agent keeps 15 percent of your earnings. But she earns her keep. For starters, an agent fights to get you a better deal than you could get on your own. In doing so, she effectively pays for herself.

Keep in mind that an agent won't necessarily represent everything you write. Here is a breakdown for how your agent is involved with your writing life.

An agent will:

- **PITCH YOUR BOOK-LENGTH WORKS**—whether fiction or non-fiction, children's or adult—to publishers who will give them serious consideration, at no cost to you. This is their primary responsibility and their specialty.
- **OFFER CAREER GUIDANCE.** An agent's job is to help you develop your brand and plan your next move.
- **NEGOTIATE YOUR CONTRACTS AND TRY TO GET YOU THE BEST TERMS.** Ninety-nine percent of the time, you will get more money for your book with an agent than without one.
- **TRY TO GET THE BEST DEAL POSSIBLE FOR YOU**—including any and all subrights sales, such as audio, film, translation rights, and more.
- **GARNER RESPONSES FROM EDITORS FASTER THAN YOU COULD ON YOUR OWN.**

An agent will not:

- **HELP YOU SELL ORIGINAL MAGAZINE ARTICLES.**
- **REPRESENT BOOKS OF POETRY.** Books of poetry are rarely traditionally published; most chapbooks available online are self-published.

WHAT IF YOU HAVE A BOOK DEAL IN HAND?

What's the correct protocol if you don't have an agent but already have a contract offer in hand from a publisher? Should you sign the contract?

Or should you try to get an agent at that point to help you negotiate the deal? That decision is yours to make—but obviously agents are very open to stepping in at that point. Says agent Laura Rennert of Andrea Brown Literary Agency, "It's fine to approach an agent [when you have a contract in hand from a publisher]. We've taken on new clients in cases where we're the first person to see the work and also in cases where there's already an offer on the table. In fact, sometimes the editor who has made the offer will recommend the author contact us. ... Agents do more than just secure an offer. They also negotiate contracts, act as the author's advocate and champion, and help the author navigate the path after publication."

THE LIFE OF AN AGENT

Ask any agent what she does on the job, and she'll tell you that she wears a lot of hats. While a newer agent may spend most of her time hunting for clients and reviewing slush-pile submissions, an experienced agent, on any given day, must deftly juggle a variety of tasks. Let's journey through the theoretical day of an agent so you can better understand her skill set and responsibilities. In no particular order, here is what an agent is doing in the office.

- **SHE PITCHES PROJECTS FROM EXISTING CLIENTS TO EDITORS.** Once an existing client has a completed manuscript or book proposal that's polished and ready, it's time for the agent to target editors and pitch the book. Much like writers carefully target and personalize their query letters to agents, the agent, in turn, carefully targets and personalizes her pitches to editors, almost all of which are done through e-mail.
- **SHE REVIEWS WORK FROM EXISTING CLIENTS AND SUGGESTS REVISIONS IF NEED BE.** As her writers pass along their newest masterpiece, an agent carefully reviews every page and detail to spot weaknesses that need to be fixed before submission. This

takes time. Looking over a 90,000-word novel with an editorial eye can take dozens of hours.

- **SHE READS INDUSTRY NEWS.** An agent needs to know when an imprint launches, an editor switches houses, or an assistant gets promoted to a crucial role. Reading trade publications such as *Publishers Weekly* (which is a good magazine for writers to peruse as well—hint, hint) lets her know what kinds of books are selling and which publishing houses are acquiring such titles. If she's part of an agency, she will work with her fellow agents to corral important news and update the agency database.

  Just as writers educate themselves about agents and their tastes, agents educate themselves about editors and *their* tastes. An agent will spend some of her time reading interviews and blogs to learn editors' personal preferences and will also peruse publishers' backlists to learn what they've already published.

- **SHE READS NEWS SOURCES OF INTEREST TO HER**—especially when they are connected to nonfiction categories she represents. Most fiction travels *toward* the agent, coming from writers through cold queries or referrals. But regarding nonfiction, it's quite common for an agent to personally seek out experts, journalists, and persons in the media to write books. For instance, if an agent sells a lot of pop-culture books, she is no doubt hunting for the next humorous blog that is on the verge of blowing up (such as the Twitter account that inspired *Sh*t My Dad Says* or the blog that led to *Texts from Dog*), hoping to turn the material into a best-selling book.

- **SHE MEETS PERSONALLY WITH PEERS AND EDITORS.** Though not as martini-heavy and glamorous as you probably picture them to be, plenty of lunch meetings still happen in New York. An agent will often get together with an editor simply to see what she's currently looking for so that the agent can funnel the most appropriate submissions to him. It's also beneficial for the agent to attend book release parties and industry gatherings when she can—again, to meet editors. I personally think of an agent as an insider, and you can't gain such a title without knowing what's going on within inner circles.

- **SHE RECEIVES OFFERS, QUESTIONS, AND REJECTIONS FROM EDITORS REGARDING MATERIAL SHE HAS ALREADY SUBMITTED.** An agent has already sent plenty of material to publishers at any given time, so responses from editors trickle in almost constantly. An editor may say yes to a project, and thus the negotiation process of nailing down "deal points" (major points, such as money) begins. The editor may also respond to a project with questions or ask for more materials—such as sequel concepts or marketing ideas. He may reply by requesting specific revisions that must be implemented if the book is to formally go to acquisitions, or he may say no outright to a project.

  If it's a particularly wonderful day, the agent may handle an auction, which is a scheduled time for multiple editors to bid for one of the agent's projects.

- **SHE FOLLOWS UP ON PAYMENTS, DEALS, AND LOOSE ENDS.** An agent chases down the latest royalty payment for your book. She nudges an editor for a response regarding a submission or question. She e-mails her contact in China to see if the sale of Mandarin language rights went through. Because an agent plays the role of middleman, she is, by definition, in the middle of a great many things, messages, deals, and happenings. Her checklist of to-dos is never small. She is your advocate.

- **SHE CONTACTS EXISTING CLIENTS WITH NEWS, THOUGHTS, CONCERNS, AND REASSURANCES.** An agent often has many clients for whom she is pitching books, as well as clients who already have published books in the marketplace. She must send a lot of different messages and keep in constant touch with each of them. She informs a client when his book reaches a bestseller list, when the publisher decides to promote his book in a magazine, or when a publisher turns down his latest project. And so on and so forth.

- **SHE FIELDS REQUESTS FOR APPEARANCES AT VARIOUS WRITING CONFERENCES AND EVENTS.** Agents are in-demand faculty members at writing conferences and retreats nationwide (and worldwide). Once an agent receives an invitation, she will initiate a conversation to work out details such as timing, travel, on-site duties, presentation topics, and critiques.
- **SHE COORDINATES WITH CO-AGENTS REGARDING SUBSIDIARY SALES.** A typical literary agent specializes in selling your *book*. Meanwhile, she works with talented co-agents to sell film rights and foreign-language rights. This means whenever she takes on a new client or a new project by an existing client, she must pass material to contacts in Hollywood and overseas, possibly scheduling a call to discuss the book and answer any questions.
- **SHE REVIEWS COLD SUBMISSIONS FROM UNKNOWN AUTHORS— AKA, TACKLING THE SLUSH PILE.** Once all of her mandatory duties (the points above) are taken care of, it's time to seek new clients and review queries. That means tackling the slush pile. While most agents review their own query letters, some have their assistants review letters. But ultimately, most assistants are there simply to weed out the worst of the worst queries (e.g., letters littered with typos or submissions that don't fit the agent's list), while the rest simply get passed on to their boss, the agent.

LITERARY AGENT ROUNDUP

THE EVOLVING ROLE AND LIFE OF AN AGENT

"I can only speak for what we do at our agency, but it's been a long time since any good agent I know has just sold books. Agenting is a full-service business and, in this day and age, when editors sometimes seem to be playing musical chairs and projects are orphaned almost as soon as they're bought, providing editorial feedback for our clients is increasingly important. We like to think

that our role is to 'cause' books to be published, and for that to happen, we need to be involved every step of the way."

—Miriam Goderich (Dystel & Goderich Literary Management)

"The biggest way in which my job has evolved in the last five years is that I've gone from building my list to solely focusing on the writers in my stable and how to make them grow. My sense is that the longer you've been in the business, the more focused your list becomes. With that in mind, the more research a querying writer does, the better. If you read up on me, for example, you will see that I am looking only for fiction, whereas if you queried me ten years ago, I was looking for memoir, pop culture, young adult, and fiction."

—Elisabeth Weed (Weed Literary)

"I entered the industry at a time of great change, so I quickly understood I would need to work closely with my authors to build their careers. In the beginning, I counseled them on the importance of having a website, using social media, and developing a general presence on the Web. I think there is a sense from authors (especially 'old-school' ones) that this is the publisher's responsibility. This may have been a role publishers had taken on at one time, but this is no longer the case. In fact, in the digital-publishing landscape, if you do not have all of these things in place, you could risk a deal, since turnaround times are much quicker with digital. As an example, I sold four or five books to digital publisher Diversion Books, and those books were released within a month. Diversion would not have bought the books if the authors had no Web presence."

—Elizabeth Kracht (Kimberley Cameron & Associates)

"One of the most obvious ways my job as an agent has evolved can be seen in how much time I spent with my clients getting their work ready for submission. Whereas I used to be able to

take a look at a manuscript or proposal and give some detailed notes and be ready to go, I now find I am digging deeper, and this can be tricky as I take on more new clients. If I really feel a project has potential, I have been asking more writers to work with independent editors and book doctors—and while this does mean money out of a client's pocket, in the long run, it is worth it. That said, I do try to offer as much one-on-one attention as I can, but this all depends on what I've got on my plate at the time. I always keep in mind that editors are looking for a reason to say no—and I do my best to find as many potential issues and smooth them out before we submit."

—J.L. Stermer (N.S. Bienstock)

NOT ALL AGENTS ARE THE SAME

Soon you'll learn how to research potential agents and markets for your work. And when you start to look at individuals up close, you'll discover that while all agents sell books, they're quite different in other ways.

For example, some agents will be very hands-on and help you edit your work, while others gravitate toward projects they believe are great as is and can be pitched immediately. Before you think that the former (a hands-on agent) is preferable to the latter, consider that she may request changes in your manuscript that you disagree with. In other words, both a "hands-on agent" and a "nonediting agent" will have their upsides and downsides.

Some agencies are well versed in the digital marketplace and the evolution of publishing. An agent at this type of agency may seek out self-published bestsellers on Amazon and may have a co-worker at the agency dedicated to helping writers build their social media presence. And for every one of these agents, another prides herself on simply finding the best writers of paperback romance (or science fiction or literary fiction) and making sure they get published—and that's it.

For every agent who is active on Twitter and has a blog that features the publishing process, there is another who keeps to herself and likes to fly under the radar. On this note, openness to submissions will vary from rep to rep. If an agent already has a full client list or has difficulty managing the size of her slush pile, she'll close herself off to submissions. Some agents take queries only from referrals or from individuals they met at a writers conference. In other words, they are not open markets to most writers, and you'll likely not be querying them. A rule of thumb to remember is that if an agent's submission info is hard or impossible to find, that's a clear sign that she's not actively seeking submissions or accepting queries. So cross her off your list, and seek out other, more available reps.

Note that agents are simply different kinds of people. If you read interviews with them and scour message boards and look at their social media, you will see if they're serious or if they love cracking jokes. Each agent has a different working style and personality, all of which can be discovered partially or completely online by reading interviews she's done or blog posts she's written, or by attending one of her conference presentations.

Lastly, know that some agents aim for only the top publishers. So let's say that you sign with an agent and she sends your novel to her ideal twelve editors at her ideal twelve publishing houses. Then, one by one, they all reject your manuscript. What now? Your agent informs you that she's sorry the book did not find a home and you should start writing your next one. She explains that she wants her clients to get published only by the best houses with the best editors and the best marketing departments and distribution plans. As agent Karen Grencik of Red Fox Literary explains, "Publishers' advances and contract terms vary substantially, and many agents simply don't think the return on their time investment is worth going to the smaller publishers." On the flip side, more and more agents are slowly becoming comfortable with selling their clients' books to e-book publishers, where print copies don't exist.

Will you be comfortable with either of these approaches? If you and your agent disagree, it may cause a rift—and your relationship will suffer. So research your agents up front (see chapter three). And if you receive an offer of representation, be sure to ask all kinds of questions that will illuminate how your (prospective) agent works.

HOW DO AGENTS MAKE MONEY?

Standard, traditional literary agents make a commission off money made from any sales related to selling your book—from royalties to an advance to other subsidiary rights. The industry standard for the agent's cut is 15 percent or less; anything more is not currently supported by the Association of Authors' Representatives.

Once you sell some rights that go beyond the standard "English-language book rights"—such as film rights, foreign-language rights, or audio rights—the agent commission becomes bigger: typically 20 percent. This is because such sales of subsidiary rights usually involve a collaborative process with co-agents in different locations, and the agents' cut must be larger, as it is now being split. For example, if you sell the film rights to your book, the agents' take of 20 percent is split between your book agent and your new book-to-film agent, with each earning 10 percent.

The only time you should ever be paying an agent out of your own pocket is for her expenses—and "recoupable expenses" (such as overnight mailings) should be spelled out in your writer-agent contract. Note how the agent is not *making* money off you here, but simply being *reimbursed*. As long as reimbursement costs are reasonable and rare, they are considered fair and standard. The good news is that because of e-mail, PDFs, and other electronic communication, a lot of these costs are being minimized.

CHAPTER TWO

BEFORE YOU PITCH

If you're a typical hot-blooded writer, you're anxious to send your work out and see what the world thinks of it. At one point or another, we've all looked at a draft for the twentieth time and thought, *If I read this thing one more time, I'm going to claw my eyeballs out.* It's at that moment that the writer throws his hands up in the air and starts querying.

But what writers must remember is that submitting work is the last and final step of their submission journey. First you have to completely finish the work. Then you have to go back and start your second draft—revising, rewriting, overhauling, cutting, adding, and more. The heart writes the first draft, but the head writes the second—and that means critical editing, where darlings will be killed. You should rewrite the manuscript once or several times to improve it and sand off the rough edges.

When you need a break, step away from the project. After you complete the first draft, take at least three weeks, if not longer, and do something else—perhaps analyze some other books you enjoy. When you come back to the manuscript with fresh eyes, you'll see all kinds of problems you didn't notice before. You can attack the work again to make it better. Repeat this process of revision and "stepping away" until you feel like you've taken it as far as you can. Then it's time to have your work critiqued by someone else.

BEFORE YOU PITCH NONFICTION

When writing a nonfiction book (anything except memoir), you do not have to finish the book before you pitch. In fact, the completed book will not be read by agents even if you send it to them.

Your key submission tool is a *nonfiction book proposal*, which explains everything about your book idea—the concept, its place in the market, the proposed design, a marketing plan, and more. Instead of a whole book, you need only three to four sample chapters from the book as well as a completed table of contents that projects the information and images you plan to include.

But before you submit that proposal, make sure your self-marketing abilities—commonly called your "writer platform"—are excellent, so you can get publishers excited about your work. (For more information about nonfiction book proposals and platform, see chapters eleven and twelve in this book.) But I stress again: Do not write the entire front-to-back text. All you need to submit is the proposal and a few chapters. Any other material likely won't be read, so keep that in mind before composing it up front.

WHEN IS YOUR SUBMISSION READY?

When is your work really *ready*? By that, I mean: When is your manuscript edited and polished to the point where you can confidently submit it to agents? I used to think that this question had no answer and that each project was so vastly different that it would be misleading to address the subject. But I was wrong.

The best answer I can give on the subject is this: *If you think your book has a problem, it does—and any book with a problem is not ready.* When I edit full-length manuscripts and then meet with writers personally to discuss my thoughts, a strange thing happens. When I address a concern in the book, the writer nods before I even finish the sentence. What this means is that he already knew about the problem and suspected it was a weak point in the story. I have simply confirmed that which he already knew.

Here are some typical concerns I run into.

- "This part where your main character gets beat up—it doesn't seem believable that so many kids just took off school like that."
- "If the main character is so stealthy, then why does he get caught by the dim-witted bad guys here?"
- "The story starts too slow. We need more action."
- "It's much too convenient that the gun just happens to appear right when the main character needs it."

In my experience, writers often know many of their issues before anyone even tells them. Which brings me back to my main point: If you think your work has a problem, then it more than likely does—and any manuscript with a problem is not ready for agent eyes. Every major problem needs to be fixed before you submit to agents. Otherwise you're just submitting a subpar work that will get rejected, and you'll lose a precious chance with those agents who say no. "Writers only get to query an agent one time with a manuscript," says agent Karen Grencik of Red Fox Literary. "There are no second chances unless an agent gives specific feedback and asks to see the revision."

When you can pass the book to beta readers or freelance editors and they point out only small issues and nitpicks—rather than major flaws—then and only then are you ready to travel to Querytown.

"If you like a work [from another author], try and understand why you like it. What are the elements that make it successful? Explore it. Don't just read. Think about it."

—Lorin Rees (Rees Literary Agency)

SEEKING CRITIQUES

Beta Readers

I can say with absolute confidence and certainty that your work will improve a little or even a lot if you simply ask for other writers' opinions. You need the eyes of other writers on your book. These fellow writers are *beta readers*: the core group of writing peers—often found in a local writing group or critique group—who will help you whip your work into shape. If such a critique group exists in your area (and one or many almost certainly do), it would behoove you to join immediately if possible.

It works like this: Beta readers will read your work, and in return you will read theirs. It's a win-win situation. First of all, you'll receive a variety of perspectives on how to improve your writing. Second, you gain insight by editing others' work. When you critique novels (or other nonfiction narratives such as memoir), you are forced to change gears from writer to editor and start seeing flaws and weak points in others' work. Then you can use that newly acquired editorial eye on your *own* work to trim and improve the writing.

When seeking beta readers, your goal is to find people who are intelligent, trustworthy, and honest. (Finding beta readers more accomplished and smarter than you is never a bad thing.) Naturally you do not have to incorporate every change a reader suggests; some ideas may legitimately be poor. But when you notice multiple beta readers making the same suggestion independent of one another, that's a key sign that you need to fix a problem before submitting to agents.

Freelance Editors

Usually writers who do not have access to an excellent cadre of beta readers turn to freelance editors for help. Employing a skilled freelance developmental book editor is a near-guaranteed way to improve your work and get helpful feedback. But you must proceed with caution. Here are six quick pieces of advice to consider when hiring a professional independent editor for your work.

1. **GET A TEST EDIT.** Hiring a freelance book doctor costs money, and you don't want to plunk down a large chunk of change before you've seen the kind of services an editor will provide. With a test edit, you send a select number of pages to the editor and have him review them. This will show you the kinds of notes and ideas the editor would make to the overall work in terms of content editing and proofreading. If you like what you see from this trial edit, then you can move forward with the entire work.

2. **LOOK FOR REFERRALS AND SUCCESS STORIES.** These days, everyone lists "freelance editor" on their qualifications. So when you're seeking out a freelance editor, seek not only an impressive bio and qualifications, but also referrals and success stories. Talk to writing peers who have used editors, and find out if they liked what they received in the exchange. And, of course, nothing succeeds like success—so look at what projects the editor has worked on that (1) got published by a traditional publisher, (2) secured literary agent representation, or (3) had notable success after being self-published.

3. **BE UP FRONT ABOUT WHAT YOU WANT FROM THE EDIT.** Know if you want an edit that's heavy on copyediting and proofreading, or an edit that will specifically analyze the pacing or tempo of your writing. Know if you want the editor to take a closer look at a section that's bothering you. If you're seeking a nonfiction book proposal edit, for instance, it might be helpful to know that you want the editor to focus on the weakest section, say, on your marketing plan and platform. If you don't give specific instruction, the editor will take a broad approach to the work.

4. **BEWARE OF ANYONE WHO CHARGES WAY TOO LITTLE OR WAY TOO MUCH.** If someone charges you $12,000 for an edit, that's way too much. If an editor offers to do everything and anything

to your 120,000-word novel for just $150, that's another red flag. Freelance editing costs depend on the book's length—and usually fall within the range of $400 to $4,000.

5. **ALWAYS SPEAK OF YOUR NOVEL IN TERMS OF BOTH WORD COUNT AND PAGES.** The font you choose and the margins you use can drastically affect page count, so always speak in terms of the novel's completed word count (e.g., 88,000 words). And if you're wondering, standard novel pages should be in 12-point Times New Roman font with standard 1" margins on all four sides.

SELF-EDITING

Sure, you'll seek out other readers to get varying opinions on your work, but don't forget the value of your own critical eye. One of the main reasons writers get rejected is that their work is simply good but not amazing. Perhaps you have a tendency to say, "At this point, I think my book is decently solid. If there are flaws, certainly an agent is willing to work with me on them."

No. That's not what agents do.

An agent's job is to sell your work and guide your career—neither of which includes editing. It's *your* job to make your work as close to spotless as you can before submitting. Sure, some agents may suggest changes and get their hands dirty with red ink and editorial suggestions. But plenty won't—and those that do help you will only provide minimal edits. So don't fall into this trap and get denied because you've submitted work that just wasn't ready.

"Don't send your book out until you can't think of any way to improve it."

—Paul Lucas (Janklow & Nesbit Associates)

How do you make sure this doesn't happen? Be a ruthless self-editor. Self-editing is a large topic, and I could spend many pages discussing it. That said, here are three simple things you can do when self-editing.

1. **BUY BOOKS ON SELF-EDITING, SUCH AS JAMES SCOTT BELL'S** *REVISION AND SELF-EDITING FOR PUBLICATION.* You can also find plenty of print guides and blog articles that will teach you basic techniques, such as eliminating excess narrative, nixing passive voice, and making sure your book starts with an interesting scene.
2. **ALWAYS BE LOOKING TO CUT.** It's much more common for a manuscript or sample chapter to have too much text than not enough. If you approach every chapter with a scalpel to trim off unnecessary words here and there, your writing will only tighten.
3. **DON'T RUSH THE PROCESS, AND PLAN ON TAKING BREAKS TO STEP AWAY.** Nothing will bring your mistakes more into focus than stepping away from the project for a time and then coming back to it. This will drastically increase your objective viewpoint.

WORD COUNT

When I travel to writers conferences, someone inevitably asks a simple, innocent question about word count—and a firestorm follows. "Standard" word count rules do exist in the publishing industry. Of course, there are always exceptions to these rules, and man, do people love pointing out the exceptions. "What about so-and-so's debut novel?" they ask. "It's sold over five million copies, and it's 175,000 words long!"

But it's important to remember that you cannot count on being the exception; you must count on being the rule. Aiming to be the exception is setting yourself up for disappointment. What some writers fail to see is that for every successful exception to the rule (e.g., a first-time 175,000-word bestseller), there are hundreds of failures. Almost always, a high word count indicates that the writer simply did not edit his work enough. Or it means he has actually written two or more books combined into one.

"But what about J.K. Rowling?" asks a man in the back of the room, putting his palms up in the air. Well—remember the first Harry Potter book? It wasn't that long. After Rowling made the publishing house oodles and oodles of money, she could do whatever she wanted. But because most writers haven't yet earned oodles, they need to stick to the rules and make sure their work gets read.

In addition to selling oodles, the other thing that can make you an exception is absolutely brilliant writing. But let's face it: Most of our work doesn't qualify as "absolutely brilliant"—and that's okay.

With these thoughts in mind, let's break down some general word count guidelines.

- **ADULT NOVELS: COMMERCIAL AND LITERARY.** Aim for between 80,000 and 89,999 words. This is a 100 percent safe range for the literary, romance, mystery, suspense, thriller, and horror genres. Now, speaking broadly, you can get away with as few as 71,000 words and as many as 109,000 words. But when a book dips below 80,000, it might be perceived as too short—it's not giving the reader enough. This range can also be applied to narrative nonfiction (also called creative nonfiction).

  The one exception to this rule is the "chick lit" genre, which favors shorter, faster reads. If you're writing chick lit, 65,000 to 75,000 is a better target range. And while it might be permissible to go over 100,000 words, if your book really warrants such length, don't cross the six-figure mark by much. Agent Rachelle Gardner of Books and Such Literary points out that more than 110,000 words is defined as "epic or saga"—and chances are your cozy mystery or literary novel is not an epic. Gardner also mentions that passing the 100,000-word mark means you've written a book that will be more costly to produce—possibly making it a difficult sell.

- **SCIENCE FICTION AND FANTASY.** Science fiction and fantasy books tend to run long, largely because of all the descriptions and world building involved. The thing is, writers tend to know that these categories run long, so they make their manuscripts run *really* long and hurt their chances with an agent. With these genres, 100,000 to 110,000 words is an excellent range. It's six figures, but it's not excessive. There's also nothing wrong with keeping it a bit shorter; it shows that you can whittle your work down. In broader terms, anything between 85,000 and 125,000 words may be acceptable.

- **MIDDLE-GRADE (MG) NOVELS.** Middle-grade fiction—that is, novels for readers in the nine-to-twelve-year-old age range— usually falls within 20,000 to 55,000 words, depending on the subject matter and target reader age. When writing a longer book aimed at twelve-year-olds (who are considered tweens), using the term "upper middle-grade" is advisable. These are books that resemble young adult fiction in matter and storytelling but tend to stick to middle-grade themes and avoid hot-button, YA-acceptable themes such as sex and drugs. With upper middle-grade, aim for 35,000 to 55,000 words. You can stray a little over but not much.

  With a simpler middle-grade idea (*Football Hero* or *Jenny Jones and the Cupcake Mystery*), aim lower. Shoot for 20,000 to 30,000 words.

- **YOUNG ADULT (YA) NOVELS.** Perhaps more than any other, YA is the one category where word count is very flexible. For starters, 55,000 to 75,000 words is a great range. The word from the agent blogosphere is that YA books are currently trending longer and can top out at 90,000 words. However, this progression is still in motion, and trends can be fickle, so you may be playing with fire the higher you go. Make sure you have a compelling reason to submit a longer story. One good reason is that your YA novel is science fiction or fantasy. Once again, these categories are expected to be a little longer because of the description and world building they entail.

On the low end, fewer than 50,000 words could be acceptable, but be sure to stay above 40,000 to remain viable in this genre.

- **PICTURE BOOKS FOR CHILDREN.** The standard word count for this category is sufficient text for twenty-eight pages, which might mean one line per page or slightly more. Aim for 500 to 600 words; if your manuscript is more than 1,000, editors and agents might shy away.

- **WESTERN.** Marketable manuscripts in this genre can be anywhere from 50,000 to 80,000 words. A good target range is anywhere around the 65,000-word mark.

- **MEMOIR.** This breed of nonfiction is queried—and evaluated by agents and editors—in much the same way a novel is, because the form relies so heavily on the writer's voice, style, approach, and story arc. Memoir is the one nonfiction category where writers usually must complete the entire manuscript prior to submitting rather than compose only a few sample chapters as part of a book proposal.

  For memoir, aim for 80,000 to 89,999 words. This is one genre where writers often have a tendency to go unnecessarily long—possibly indicating to an agent that they're too close to their own story to properly revise their work. With that in mind, a lower word count (70,000 to 79,999) is not a terrible thing. If you must go longer than the suggested range, don't exceed 99,999.

- **NONFICTION.** Outside of "novel-like" books such as memoir and narrative nonfiction that fall into the same 70,000 to 100,000 frame work, the nonfiction categories do not abide by word count guidelines. That's because the word count completely depends on the type of book you're writing. A book full of humorous dog photos, for instance, may have 1,000 words of text or fewer. A true-crime book may run 60,000 words or 100,000, depending on the subject matter. A niche book about the history of Cuban art in Miami could be any length depending on how much narrative and text accompanied the art.

When you pitch nonfiction, you do so with a book proposal in which you'll have to estimate the completed word count. To do this, you must envision what the final product will be like and, if necessary, use other published books as reference points.

Other Word Count Thoughts

Some literary agents, such as Kristin Nelson of Nelson Literary Agency, say that you shouldn't think about word count but rather about telling the best story possible at the right pace. While she's technically correct, not every agent feels that way. Many aren't willing to give a 129,000-word debut novel a shot. Agents receive so many queries and submissions that they often look for reasons to say no. And if you submit a project well outside the typical length conventions, then you are giving them ammunition to reject you.

Some writers may just take their chances, cross their fingers, and hope for the best. But I believe that you cannot count on being the exception; you must count on being the rule. That's the way to give yourself the best shot at success.

REMEMBER THAT YOUR BOOK IS YOUR BOOK, NOT SOMEONE ELSE'S

When it comes to word count, writers are often tempted to point to another story—such as some Stephen King novels—and think, *That person did it, so why can't I?*

Beware, beware, beware that line—it's a misguided attempt at rationale and justification, and it gets writers in trouble every day. Keep in mind that your book is a *book*—not something else. And it's written by *you*—not King or [insert best-selling author]. To keep you grounded and focused, here are some important things to remember as you craft and submit your work.

1. **YOUR BOOK IS NOT A MOVIE.** Films are a visual medium, whereas books are not. Film studios may possess oodles of money to spend on promotion; your publishing house likely won't. So if a blockbuster movie decides to spend the first ten minutes following around the bad guy rather than the protagonist, that doesn't mean your debut novel can do the same. If a movie decides to start slow with a lot of sweeping shots over a landscape, that doesn't mean your debut novel can do the same. Don't rationalize an unwise writing choice simply because films can get away with it.

2. **REMEMBER THAT YOU'RE NOT A BEST-SELLING AUTHOR YET.** Best-selling authors like Dan Brown have reached a point of success where they can do anything they want. For example, take a look at Brown's *The Lost Symbol*, in which the first chapter features a main character waking up from a dream. Almost all agents dislike this "wake up from a dream" tactic to start a book. But Brown can get away with it because his books are guaranteed to sell, no matter what. Your book does not begin with such guarantees. Agent Barbara Poelle of Irene Goodman Literary Agency says it politely: "When you have a résumé like Stephen King's, readers trust that the work will deliver. This allows authors of that echelon to take risks … ."

3. **THE CURRENT YEAR IS NOT 1936 OR 1954 OR 1979, NOR WILL IT EVER BE AGAIN.** The classic *Moby-Dick* has extremely long chapters and passages with nothing but internal narration.

The classic *Gone with the Wind* is more than twice the length of today's average debut novel. Just because a novel from decades or centuries ago was able to employ certain narrative techniques doesn't mean you should emulate it in your work. Today's average reader has dozens of mediums vying for his attention, from TV shows to cat videos on the Internet. That means modern books start faster and trend shorter than in the past. Sure, you can look to the past for writing guidance and excellence, but you should focus on reading *contemporary* books—especially debuts by peers in your genre—so you understand what agents and editors are looking for *now.*

CHAPTER THREE

RESEARCH REPS AND

CREATE YOUR LIST

Once your book is finished, it's time to start submitting to agents. Start by creating a new Microsoft Word or Excel document so you can keep detailed track of your submissions, target agents, resource materials, and more. This document will help you personalize query letters, find more agents to contact, and know when to follow up on submissions.

Now it's time to create your list of potential agents to query. As you start compiling agent names and contact info, think in terms of casting a wide net. Scour databases and websites (we'll explore these later in the chapter) to put together the largest possible collection of reps to contact; then start narrowing it down. Understand right off the bat that not every agent is for you. You'll be targeting only a fraction of the active reps out there—seeking those who represent the specific type of book you're writing.

CLASSIFYING YOUR WORK

Before you go looking for agents to contact, you must define what you've written. In other words, when push comes to shove, you have to classify it as *something.* So what type of book is it? (Note that fiction is broken down into *genres,* while nonfiction is broken down into *categories.* If you're confused about genre and category definitions, see the Glossary of Genres and Category Definitions in the Appendix.)

Some writers will have no difficulty with this step—immediately telling their friends that they've written a romance or a thriller or an illustrated picture book. But other writers will not be so sure. They'll question the exact classification of their work and therefore won't know which agents to target. Let's run through some examples of category dilemmas.

1. **YOU'VE WRITTEN A LEGAL THRILLER AND CAN'T FIND MANY AGENTS WHO REPRESENT THIS TYPE OF BOOK.** Your mistake is that you're specifically looking for agents seeking "legal thrillers" when you should just be looking for agents seeking "thrillers." A popular fiction genre—such as thriller—has many subcategories, including techno-thrillers, medical thrillers, legal thrillers, climate fiction thrillers ("cli-fi"), and more. But most agents won't get into the nitty-gritty when explaining what categories they want. They'll just say, "I seek thrillers." And anyone who says that is a potential market for your thriller. Some will personally lean toward your subgenre of thriller, while others won't. You won't know exactly which subcategories they prefer, so just query all available markets and hope for the best. Also, it's likely that a few agents out there will mention their admiration for "legal thrillers" in their personal information. If you see an agent put out a call for the exact type of book you're writing, that's a great potential match for you. When querying, you can say, "Because I've read that you are actively seeking [x], I thought you might enjoy my novel, [*Title*]."

2. **YOU'VE WRITTEN A SCIENCE FICTION YOUNG ADULT BOOK AND DON'T KNOW WHETHER TO CONTACT YOUNG ADULT AGENTS OR SCIENCE FICTION AGENTS.** The answer is to query young adult agents. If it's a book for kids, it's a book for kids. It's not like young adult romance should be treated like adult romance. If it's fundamentally YA or MG you should query agents in those categories.

3. **YOU'RE NOT SURE IF YOUR BOOK IS SUSPENSE OR THRILLER BECAUSE IT BLENDS THE TWO.** You won't find many agents who put out a call for "a crossbreed of thriller and suspense." Instead you'll get a lot of agents simply asking for "thriller" and some asking for "suspense." Feel free to query all of them. In your contact letter to a specific agent, you can alternate between the classification terms, depending on what her needs are. Or you can just query them all, stating up front that your book is a "suspenseful thriller."

4. **YOU'RE WRITING IN A CATEGORY OF FICTION THAT SOME AGENTS MAY REP, BUT VIRTUALLY NONE REQUEST IT SPECIFICALLY IN THEIR GUIDELINES.** If you're dealing with a "lonely" genre of fiction, such as "humorous fiction" or "medieval fiction," and can't find many target reps for the book, you can always seek out *generalists*. Some agents will be very specific concerning what they want and don't want. But plenty of reps will instead say something like "I'm open to any area of fiction that's done well." If an agent publicly says she has no restrictions concerning submissions, feel free to contact her and hope for the best. This problem of writing in an under-the-radar category is even more common with nonfiction; it can be difficult to find an agent specifically asking for "books about Wicca" or "books about exterminating unwanted pests from your home." If you're writing nonfiction like this, your strategy, again, should be to seek generalists or to bypass the agent and go straight to a publisher.

5. **YOU'VE WRITTEN A NOVEL THAT DOESN'T FIT INTO ANY SO-CALLED GENRE.** Some novels will be easy to categorize, such as fantasies, Westerns, and horror. But what about novels that do not fit into any of these popular commercial genres? Chances are, you're going to categorize them as "literary fiction" or "mainstream fiction." Literary novels do not fall into any popular genre type, focus on character more than plot, and value impressive voice, style, and technique. Mainstream fiction is a similar category, but the term is used to describe nongenre stories that have mass appeal and can transcend fans of literary fiction and appeal to members of book clubs.

"If you are unable to tell me what it is you're writing (and do not say you 'really can't' because 'it has never been done before,' because every time an author says that, a kitten explodes), then how am I going to frame it and sell it? There are of course subgenres within genres, but an author straddling too many genres is akin to Sharktobear lurching out of the ocean, growling and biting and thrashing its eight arms hither and thither. And no one wants to approach that—not an agent, not a publisher, and not Greenpeace."

—Barbara Poelle (Irene Goodman Literary Agency)

FINDING AGENTS

If you were looking for an electrician to repair your house, you'd turn to the Yellow Pages and Google. Well, finding literary agents isn't much different. You'll use print resources as well as the Internet in your quest. By this point, you now understand what you're writing (the genre or category term) and can therefore spot agents who are looking for what you're writing.

Concerning print resources (and naturally, as the editor, I'm biased), seek out the most recent edition of the *Guide to Literary Agents*, a huge print directory of agents that comes out every year. It's the biggest book database of agents available in print. And if you have the latest *GLA* and want more, here are other resources to consider.

Print Resources

- *Jeff Herman's Guide to Book Publishers, Editors and Literary Agents* (annual)
- *The Christian Writer's Market Guide* (annual, specializes in religious markets)
- *The Canadian Writer's Market* (annual, specializes in Canadian markets)

Online Resources

- Writersmarket.com[1] (pay site)
- Publishermarketplace.com (pay site)
- Querytracker.com (free)
- Aaronline.org/MAgents (free)

DOES AN AGENT'S LOCATION MATTER?

If you imagine that all literary agents live and work in New York City, you wouldn't be far from the truth. About 75 percent of them work in the greater NYC metropolitan area. So does that mean agents outside of The Big Apple don't have the skill, clout, and connections to be effective?

No, not at all. Plenty of agents operate in other parts of the country. You can find many in Washington, DC, the Colorado area, and up and

---

1. Writersmarket.com is also helmed by Writer's Digest. All the other resources listed here have no affiliation with WD.

down the West Coast. The simple truth is that an agent's location doesn't matter. All that matters is that editors pick up the phone when she calls. You can judge the capability of a Texas agent the same way as you judge the capability of a New York agent. Examine her background; make sure she has some sort of publishing experience—such as editorial experience or apprenticeship as an agent—and see if she's currently selling books. The last one is key. If she's selling books to legitimate, quality publishers, then her skill is tested and approved. You can see what books an agent has sold by looking at her website or checking Publishers marketplace.com.

That said, it's not quite this simple when dealing with agents based in other countries—specifically the United Kingdom and Canada. If you're based in the United States, you should query U.S. agents. If you're based in the United Kingdom, you should query U.K. agents first and U.S. agents second. If you're based in Canada, you should query both Canadian and American agents.

RESEARCHING FURTHER

Beyond these basic resources, try some simple social media, and you'll be amazed at what turns up. If you get on Twitter and start following several literary agents, the site will begin suggesting other agents for you to follow. You'll quickly find hundreds of them on the site—and you can examine each to determine whether she's a potential match for your work. At some point, you'll find yourself on message boards or other websites—such as Querytracker.com or Guidetoliteraryagents.com/blog—where agent news and updates are passed around. These sites are excellent resources for finding potential matches.

Scour high and low, and start composing a grand list—but that's just the first step. Once you've created your initial list of target agents, it's time to do a little (or a lot of) research on each agent. Do some intelligence gathering on Twitter. Read her blog. Scan interviews she's done.

Check her official agency website. All of this research will likely illuminate many interesting personal and professional tidbits that will help with your submission.

Consider these hypothetical examples.

- An agent's website says she accepts "all genres of fiction." However, the website also lists ten of her favorite novels of all time. All of them could be considered "literary, character-driven" tales.

    WHAT THIS MEANS FOR YOU: While some agents are indeed open to "any fiction," the truth is that the fiction genre spectrum—as well as the nonfiction category spectrum—is vast, and her passions likely lie in *some* specific areas here and there. These favorite novels all fit a certain mold, and the agent is showing you the type of novel she truly loves. If your novel shares some aspects of her favorites, that means she's a great fit for your book.

- On Twitter, an agent explains she is currently on a temporary hiatus from reviewing queries.

    WHAT THIS MEANS FOR YOU: It means you shouldn't query her right now, naturally. If you didn't check her Twitter, you would have submitted to a black hole and received no reply, likely equating it with a rejection when it wasn't. Keep checking her Twitter feed until she announces that she is open to submissions again.

- Remarkably, you can't find any social media for an agent, nor can you locate any online interviews for her.

    WHAT THIS MEANS FOR YOU: She likely doesn't actively seek new clients. Most agents are game for an interview or happy to attend a local writers conference. But some agents don't do basic outreach such as that, and they may not even have a website or a submissions e-mail you can find online. This almost certainly means that they are so established with their existing clients and referrals that they do not accept unsolicited queries from writers.

- In an interview, an agent explains that she represents science fiction but specifically wants "earth-based sci-fi adventures."

  Or: At a writers conference, an agent on a panel wonders aloud why no one has pitched her a book about old drive-in movie theaters.

  Or: On her blog about agenting and publishing, an agent has a "wish list" where she lists the exact types of stories she wishes she could find in the slush pile—such as "an Indiana Jones adventure with a teenage female protagonist."

  WHAT THIS MEANS FOR YOU: These are great examples of *agent specificity*. Lots of times, agents make public their genres and categories of interest without much explanation or fanfare. In interviews online or on their blogs, agents have more room to get specific and tell you more. This is important, because while an agent may seem like a loose match, a closer look may reveal that while she represents mystery, she gravitates away from the subgenre of mystery you're writing. Remember that individual agents don't always have the easiest time updating their info on different websites or even possibly their own agency website (if they are one agent of many), so it's important to check out a variety of sources to dig deeper.

YOUR FINISHED LIST OF AGENTS

While your list will be ever growing and evolving, at some point you should feel comfortable with your list of potential reps and the research you've done on them, and you can query them with confidence. All your research has provided you with valuable "connection" lines that help you personalize each query and validate your reason for contacting that agent. You know which agents have put out a call for exactly what you're writing versus which agents aren't specific but may be seeking what you write. You have your list, and the list is likely broken down into tiers.

Now it's time to start querying. And don't worry—we have several chapters and oodles of Q&A coming up on how to query effectively. But there's one question that comes up even before the finer points of writing a query: "If I do have a small list of 'ideal agents,' is it wise to query them all at once?" This decision is up to you. If you truly feel like your manuscript and query have been polished and battle-tested by independent editors, then you have nothing to fear. Query all your ideal agents at once. On the other hand, if you're not sure, then it's probably wise *not* to query your handful of ideal agents at the same time—because your work may have a flaw that will need to be fixed in the middle of the submission process.

SHOULD YOU SIGN WITH A NEW AGENT?

THE CONS

- New agents are likely less experienced in contract and money negotiations, and thus in a weaker position to demand a high advance or better contract terms.
- They likely know fewer editors than a rep who's been in business a while, meaning there is a less likely chance they can help you get published.
- It may take longer for a new agent to get responses from editors, and thus the submission process can be slower than it would be otherwise.
- New literary agents come, and some go. If your agent is in business for a year and doesn't find the success for which she hoped, she could bail on the biz altogether. That leaves you without a home. If you sign with an agent who's been in business for fourteen years, however, chances are she won't quit tomorrow.

THE PROS

- They are actively building their client list—and that means they're hungry to sign new writers.

- They're usually willing to give your work a longer look. They may even be willing to work with you on a project to get it ready for submission.
- You will probably get more attention than you would with an established rep—during every stage of the process.
- Just as they may have little going for them, they also have little working against them. An established agent once told me that a new agent is in a unique position because she has no duds under her belt.

If you can't make up your mind about a new agent who offers you representation, use your phone call with them to ask questions (see chapter thirteen) and make a final decision. If she works within a larger agency, she can rely on fellow agents to provide contacts, suggestions, and guidance. Says agent Katharine Sands of the Sarah Jane Freymann Literary Agency: "An agent with little or no sales who has been an assistant at a leading agency will have just as much clout getting to an editor perhaps as an established agent, at least initially. One of the things I always advise writers to do is to ask an interested agent—that is, one who's made an offer of representation—'Why do you want to be my agent?' They will then hear a very clear thumbnail sketch of how that agent will sound agenting."

THE FOUR OTHER WAYS TO CONTACT AGENTS (BESIDES QUERIES)

Although the process of following submission guidelines and writing a query letter is tedious and sometimes frustrating, it is, statistically speaking, the number one way to get an agent to sign with you. Kristin Nelson of Nelson Literary Agency once surveyed more than two hundred published authors and asked them how they came to sign with their agent, and more than 60 percent explained that it was a cold query through the slush pile.

That said, a query letter is not the sole way to get your work in front of agents. There are four other acceptable routes you can use. In fact, a certain percentage of agents in publishing actually close themselves off to cold queries altogether and only accept submissions through the "side door" methods listed below—so review them closely. Please note that even if you take one of these alternative methods to get your work read, the agent may ask you to send a query when you send your manuscript, so a good letter is still of the utmost importance.

1. **CONTESTS.** Agents sometimes judge online contests. Oftentimes websites will host writing competitions—such as for the first page of a horror manuscript or a pitch paragraph for a memoir, etc. The agent reviews the entries and sees your pitch or writing during the contest. If she likes what she sees, she will contact you and request more material.

   Don't believe me? Take Tamar Rydzinski of the Laura Dail Literary Agency. She judged a previous installment of the "Dear Lucky Agent" Contest on my *Guide to Literary Agents* blog. It was a free contest where people submitted the first page of their unpublished young adult novel. Her top three winners won an agent critique from her. Tamar was so impressed by one winner that she asked to see the full novel. Soon after, Tamar offered representation to the writer and sold the writer's novels in a two-book deal.

   So whenever you see an agent-judged contest—especially if it's free—jump in and see what happens! You could win a critique and even find your agent match.

2. **CRITIQUES.** Agents sometimes do critiques as part of a conference or an online class. A critique is a straightforward way to get your writing in front of an agent's eyes. At minimum, you'll get helpful feedback, but if she likes what she sees, you may find a connection.

To give you another example, Writer's Digest runs instructional webinars each week, usually with an agent instructor. Typically each attendee gets a critique from the agent to help make his or her work better. As with the contests, if the agent really likes what she sees, she'll request more. So far, at least five agents have signed clients after reading their work as part of a Writer's Digest webinar.

3. **REFERRALS.** When you query an agent, normally your e-mail lands in her in-box (the slush pile). It's reviewed quickly as the agent tries to assess whether your writing or the story seems good enough for her to invest more time. In other words, submitting to a slush pile means your work will get a quick look, and the turnaround time for a response is very hit and miss. Neither of these factors is ideal. Getting a referral changes all that.

A referral is when an agented writer passes your work to his agent with a stamp of approval. Referrals are often read soon after they arrive—pushed nearer the top of the agent's to-do list. If one of the agent's authors is giving this new writer a thumbs-up, the agent will likely take a longer look at his work, going beyond what she would do for an average submission. I've heard multiple agents say something along the lines of "Good writers travel in packs," so referrals make the agent's job easier—that helps you avoid the slush pile.

So seek out referrals from any individuals you feel comfortable asking. Let's say that you join a local writing group and a few of the writers there already have agents and published books. Perhaps one of those writers agrees to critique your novel or proposal. If he really enjoys it, he may offer to submit it to his agent. If the fellow writer's response is positive but he doesn't offer a referral, you can gently ask for one, provided you feel like you're not overstepping any bounds. The worst the writer can say is no.

4. **WRITERS CONFERENCES.** Every year, there are approximately 125 writers conferences held in the United States and Canada. Many of those have literary agents in attendance, and those agents attend specifically to meet with writers one-on-one and hear pitches. Many times, the agents aren't even making any money to attend events—so the key upside of their attending is to find that diamond in the rough who's got an amazing book up his sleeve.

I found my own literary agent at a conference. I speak at about ten writing events per year, and beyond simply finding an agent, I believe conferences are a great opportunity to immerse oneself in the business side of publishing. You meet editors; you make writing friends for life; you get instruction; your creativity is refreshed; you find inspiration from others who have succeeded. But perhaps most of all, you get the chance to meet agents in person, look them in the eye, and talk to them about your book.

"Go to writers conferences! Conferences are where the art of writing and the business of publishing intersect. They're great places to network and become part of a larger writing community. And they give writers incredible access to the insights of top editors and literary agents. I've had the good luck of meeting several of my clients at conferences. Having that face-to-face contact can tell you so much about how you will work with someone."

—Elizabeth Evans (Jean V. Naggar Literary Agency)

Here are some dos and don'ts for pitching to agents at a writers conference.

Conference Dos

1. Do practice your pitch in advance.

2. Do be able to explain what your book is about in one sentence. (This is called a *log line*.)

3. Do go to as many educational sessions as possible to learn from authors, agents, and editors—and take notes. You'll get insights that help to perfect your book and your pitch, and you may get insights about which agents would be a good fit for your book.

4. Do bring business cards in case an agent asks for one.

5. Do your best to be friendly and open. Smile.

6. Do dress the part. You don't need a fancy dress or a three-piece suit. But don't come looking like you just woke up. Remember that an agent is looking for a business partner.

7. Do bring some extra cash. The conference will likely have a book store, and you might also want to schmooze and make writer friends at the hotel bar. Occasionally these social events attract agents, but they're also great places to meet writers who can give you referrals.

8. Do read other writers' blog posts describing their experiences at conferences so you can get a better sense of how to best spend your time. Especially seek out writers who've met with agents at the conference in previous years.

9. Do seek out conferences that focus on your specialty, if applicable. There are specialty writers conferences for scribes of children's books, thriller/mystery, romance, and Christian works.

Conference Don'ts

1. Don't pass agents or editors any pages. Agents can't carry around sample pages from all the writers they meet. They'd collapse from all that weight, and it would make their suitcase explode.

2. Don't come in with a long, rambling pitch. Aim to discuss your book and yourself in ninety seconds.

3. Don't skimp. Most conferences charge a base fee to attend, and then they charge for add-ons, including pitching to agents, receiv-

ing critiques, or seeing the evening keynote speaker. If you can swing it money-wise, take advantage of all aspects that you believe can help you. It's worth money to be face to face with an agent.

4. Don't be afraid to start conversations—whether with industry professionals or fellow scribes. Be bold, but use your best judgment. Don't pitch an agent in the bathroom or interrupt someone's conversation to step in and introduce yourself. Creating such an awkward moment will work against you.

5. Don't monopolize an agent's time. If you sit down at a table and an agent joins you and others, know that most if not all of the people next to you will want to chat with the agent. So be respectful, and do not dominate her attention for long periods of time. Hogging an agent's time doesn't make a good impression.

To find writers conferences, start by consulting market resources such as *Guide to Literary Agents* and asking local writing groups if they sponsor annual events in the area. Also note that simply using Google is an underrated approach. Try Googling your regional area(s) and the words "writers conference," and see what comes up. Just this moment, I searched for "Virginia writers conference" as a sample. Within the first two pages of search results, I turned up events in Roanoke, Virginia Beach, Hampton Roads, and Richmond. Not bad at all.

You'll find that there are general writers conferences out there, as well as events that have a particular focus—such as children's books (Society of Children's Book Writers and Illustrators [SCBWI]), mystery writing (Mystery Writers of America [MWA]), romance (Romance Writers of America [RWA]), Christian writing, screenwriting, and journalism (Society of Professional Journalists [SPJ]).

If you have a completed manuscript, look for an event that has not only a sizeable number of agents attending, but more specifically, a good amount of professionals seeking the genre/category you're writing. Money should and will factor in, so make sure this specific conference will be worth it. If you attend a large conference and pay $600 to schmooze with twenty agents, it won't be of much help if only one or two will consider that travel memoir you've composed.

Remember that there are many events nationwide vying for your attendance, so take your time and choose wisely.

LITERARY AGENT ROUNDUP ›
WRITERS CONFERENCE PITCHING TIPS

"Relax. We are people, too, and we are there because we want to meet you and find someone to represent. Some conferences do a better job than others in preparing writers for these things, but just remember to be yourself. Act professionally, and remember: The more relaxed you can be about things, the better for both parties."

—Elisabeth Weed (Weed Literary)

"Make sure I represent your genre to make the best use of your money and time. If you encounter an agent [including me] that dismisses you because they don't handle your genre, ask if you can practice your pitch or ask their general advice. I suggest every writer take advantage of agents at conferences, even if your work isn't ready; this is good practice, and an agent may ask to see your work when it's ready. Many of the writers I have signed I have met at pitch sessions. My best advice is to practice and hone your pitch well before you attend the conference. Practice out loud [and] in front of people, and practice a shortened version in case we meet in the elevator. A composed, professional-appearing author will live on in my mind. Focusing your pitch on plot, themes, and premise will help you communicate it effectively. Never pitch an agent in the bathroom, and avoid it at lunch and dinner tables if you are seated next to one at a conference—unless asked. For those conferences where they work me hard, meals are my

downtime. Be mindful of personal boundaries, and try not to monopolize an agent's attention in a group setting."

—Elizabeth Kracht (Kimberley Cameron & Associates)

"Don't read from a page in your notebook! If I ask you what your book is about and you can't tell me the plot in a concise, compelling way without reading word for word from your notebook, then don't bother."

—Jennifer De Chiara (Jennifer De Chiara Literary)

"First, some authors don't seem to understand their true 'hook,' or [the] most interesting aspect of their work. One writer I met spoke about his young adult fantasy novel, but it wasn't until the end of his pitch that he mentioned how his book was inspired by Japanese folklore and myths. How cool! That is what I would have wanted to hear first. Until then, it sounded like just another young adult fantasy. Second: Some authors overpraise their work. Some people told me how wonderful, great, amazing, funny, etc., their projects are. Coming from the author, such statements make me a bit skeptical. Of course the writer thinks his or her own work is amazing, but what is it about your work that makes it so fabulous? Why is it wonderful? I want more concrete information about an author's work so I can really think about where the book might fit in the market."

—Taryn Fagerness (Taryn Fagerness Agency)

On what not to do at a conference: "There's sort of a running joke between agents about writers who will pitch you at a conference while you're in the bathroom. It's funny, because no matter how many times you hear about it happening to someone else, you always think, That really won't happen to me. Then it does."

—Suzie Townsend (New Leaf Literary and Media)

"I love when someone meets me with a big smile. Always take a deep breath before you approach an agent—and smile. This makes me feel relaxed and in turn will make the author feel relaxed—and that is the only way you are able to really connect and share your story. I've had authors sit down with something to prove or even with a bit of anger or defensiveness. This does not work. I spend most of my time trying to deflect this energy, and it takes away from the purpose of the meeting. Keep in mind that we are here to meet you, and we are hoping to find a match."

—J.L. Stermer (N.S. Bienstock)

"Relax; make it conversational ... . Try to condense your pitch into the equivalent of a pitch letter or jacket flap copy. Anything longer is unnecessary for the limited time. Leave time to discuss."

—Stacey Glick (Dystel & Goderich)

CHAPTER FOUR

THE SUBMISSION PROCESS:

WHAT TO EXPECT AT A GLANCE

The time has come. Your novel or memoir or book proposal (we'll talk more about book proposals in chapter eleven) is now complete. Not only is it complete; you've revised it several times and incorporated the critical ideas of peers and editors to make it better. You've developed a list of agents to target and researched each one.

You're *ready*. It's time to start the submission process and send out your work.

"Please don't query with unfinished fiction! What if I like what you've sent me and I request the full manuscript? You won't have anything ready. When agents are interested in your pitch and ask to see the full manuscript, we want to be able to read it right away. So don't pitch until the whole thing sparkles."

—Linda Epstein (Jennifer De Chiara Literary)

So what materials do you send to agents so they'll consider repping your books? The short answer is: It all depends on what they ask for.

All agents want similar components, but each may want a different configuration of them. Some only want a query letter, which is a one-page letter that typically begins all correspondence. Some want a query and a synopsis. Some nonfiction agents want a proposal right away. Some don't. Some want print queries via snail mail. Some want only e-mailed submissions with a certain word in the subject line. The key is to just give them what they want how they want it.

If you're writing fiction, an agent will most likely ask for your query. At some point, they may follow up and ask for your synopsis and all or part of your manuscript. A few may ask for a short bio as well. For non-fiction, the book proposal and query are the central pieces. Those are the main weapons at your disposal. Even though each agent may differ in what she requests and how she requests it, if you have the basic, polished pieces, you're in business.

FOLLOW SUBMISSION GUIDELINES

Just like magazine editors and book publishers, literary agents have submission guidelines concerning how writers should contact them. These guidelines communicate everything you need to know to pass along work for consideration. Agents are usually good about keeping their guidelines clear and making them available. They do this because when writers know what they want and how they want it, there are fewer misdirected queries clogging their in-box. So remember to follow guidelines exactly. A dirty truth about agents is that, because of their constantly overwhelming workload, many of them are looking for any reason to say no to your submission simply to cut their humungous pile down by one. Don't give them that reason. Honor their requests.

"It's important to follow submission guidelines, because honoring such a basic request shows a willingness to work as a team with an agent."

—Dawn Frederick (Red Sofa Literary)

An agent's posted submission guidelines typically break down into three parts.

1. **A LIST OF ALL THE GENRES AND CATEGORIES OF BOOKS THE AGENT REPRESENTS AND THEREFORE WANTS TO RECEIVE FROM WRITERS.** If you want to know what types of books an agent represents, she'll tell you. Sometimes agents can be broad in their list of desired genres, and that's where further research comes in handy. Interviews and past sales can help illuminate exactly what kind of books they like and sell. Some agents will be willing to review dozens of genres and categories, whereas others specialize in something specific (such as picture books for kids).

2. **INSTRUCTIONS ON HOW TO SUBMIT WORK FOR REVIEW.** Remember that each agent will want materials sent in a different way, and she'll be forthright about it in her guidelines, so take note and do what she asks. Some agents may want the word *Query* in the subject line of the e-mail. Some may want materials attached to the e-mail, whereas others demand they be pasted into the e-mail itself. Some may request that you include return postage if you contact them via postal mail and not the Internet.

3. **HOW AND WHEN WRITERS SHOULD EXPECT TO HEAR BACK.** In addition to learning how to reach out to an agent, submission guidelines often include information about how an agent will get back to you with some kind of answer. For example, "Responds to queries within eight weeks." Sadly, these guidelines have evolved over the past five years: Silence is becoming a common answer.

Many agents now say things like, "If you do not hear back from us in six weeks, please consider that a no." This is an attempt by agents to save time by not sending thousands of rejections each year. This way, they can direct their energies elsewhere.

These intricacies make it critical for all querying writers to keep a detailed spreadsheet of agents and guidelines so they can keep track of who wants a query only, who requires snail mail, and when those six weeks have passed, for instance.

You can find agents' guidelines in resources such as *Guide to Literary Agents* and in some of their interviews online. But no matter where you get information on agents' guidelines as you research, whether from print sources or online, you'll want to check the official agency website as the final step before contacting them. This allows you to: (1) make sure the submission instructions did not change yesterday (the agency website is the first source that gets updated, along with their Twitter profile) and (2) be sure an agent is still at that agency and did not switch agencies or go on maternity leave the week before.

THE IMPORTANCE OF SIMULTANEOUS SUBMISSIONS

Once you're ready to dive in headfirst, a simple question emerges: Can you query multiple literary agents at the same time? Absolutely. This is both normal and encouraged. The simple fact is that an agent may take three months to get back to you, and then her response may simply be a form rejection. That's no way to go about getting a book published. You must cast a net—but don't cast a terribly wide net.

So how many agents should you contact at one time? Would it be wise to just mail out your query to all agents who rep science fiction at once? I wouldn't. I would submit to six to eight at a time, including those you've met at a writers conference or retreat.

I say six to eight because I want you to protect yourself. What if you submit your query to all agents on your master list, but—heaven forbid—your query letter stinks? Every agent will turn you down, and you'll have hit a brick wall at the beginning of your journey. Instead, submit to a limited number of agents and gauge the response. If you submit to seven agents and get seven rejections with no reps asking to see more work, then guess what? Your query stinks. So edit it. Overhaul it. Give it to friends, beta readers, and maybe a professional book editor for a look.

This concept holds true throughout the submission process. Let's say that you send your polished query to seven more literary agents and get four responses asking for more work. Congratulations—your query letter is doing its job. But none of those four agents who see a partial ask to read your full manuscript. Guess what that means? Your first few chapters aren't up to snuff. Revise them. Overhaul them. Give the chapters to friends for a blunt critique. Remember that agents will almost never reply with a personalized rejection detailing where your story went wrong. It's up to you to figure out why you're falling short.

"Always follow submission guidelines to a tee (from the requested material to how long you should wait to follow up). And be prepared for the next step before submitting anything. Make sure you've got all the material an agent might request—a finished and revised full manuscript, information about your previous publishing history, and a synopsis—on hand and at the ready to send, should an agent ask to see that material after reading your query."

—Mollie Glick (Foundry Literary + Media)

If you think six to eight is actually too *many* to send to, remember that 99 percent don't necessarily want to review the query exclusively. Agents are aware that authors target multiple reps at once, so (unless the agent specifically asks to know) your query doesn't need to say, "This is a simultaneous submission."

The only instance in which you'll submit to fewer than six to eight is if you want to entice an agent with the news that your query is exclusive. This is a risk, so make sure the agent knows what you're doing, or it's all a waste of time. When you send the e-query, have the subject line read, "Query Exclusive for [Agent Name]: [BOOK TITLE]." Then repeat in your query letter's first lines that you are querying this agent exclusively and why. Drive the message home. The hope is that this will stir the agent to action and that she will treat your submission as a top priority for review. Most will read it soon, as they realize that an exclusive query is a rare thing. If the agent does not respond within three to four weeks, it's time to move on and query others.

DEALING WITH REJECTION

Unfortunately the high that comes when you begin formal submissions might quickly be dampened if rejections start trickling in. The truth is that rejection is a natural and necessary part of the submission process. An agent can't just like the work or even like it a lot—she has to *love love love* the book to take it on. Slowly but surely casting a wide net gives you best chance of generating that bolt of lightning between you and an agent.

> *"It's an incredibly subjective business—something which is very important to keep in mind if and when the rejection letters start pouring in. There are a ton of good agents out there, and oftentimes it's just finding the one who is the best fit."*
>
> —Andrea Somberg (Harvey Klinger, Inc.)

There are different ways agents will reject writers. Like I mentioned, the "silent rejection" is unfortunately becoming more popular. Then there is the "form rejection" pasted into a reply. And finally there is the elusive yet immensely valuable "personalized rejection," when an agent takes the time to address you and your work in the reply. Because it would take many hours out of each week, agents can only give personal rejections to 1 to 10 percent of all the work they turn down. If you do get a personalized rejection, review that agent's thoughts and notes closely. You're essentially getting a free critique. Another reason personalized rejections are interesting is that they are often an unspoken invitation to submit your book again if you implement the agent's suggested changes (though this is not always the case).

No matter what kind of rejection you receive, nothing good can come from getting angry or defensive. Rather than shooting off a half-baked attack at the agent, your time is much better spent finding a new market to query or determining whether your writing still needs work.

If you do receive some nos, you can take comfort knowing countless writers before you went down this same path before finding success. Kathryn Stockett, author of *The Help*, claims that sixty agents said no before one fell in love with her novel. The first Harry Potter book was rejected more than ten times. John Grisham's first novel was turned down forty-five times before someone said yes. The list goes on—so do not lose heart. Successful authors meet rejection with more hard work. As Stockett collected her rejections for *The Help*, she continued to rewrite and revise the novel to help her chances, and that probably was the reason she found success in the end.

"An agent is looking for a personal connection to a story. The best fit is an agent who loves the story as much as the author does, either because her life experience is similar to that of the storyline or because the story adds dimension to the agent's understanding of the world, and that will give an agent the incentive to do the hard work necessary to find a manuscript the right home."

—Karen Grencik (Red Fox Literary)

SUBMISSION CHECKLIST

- Most of your correspondence will be electronic, and while there is a tendency to be less formal over e-mail, resist that habit. Address the agent as you would in a paper letter—be formal. Casual elements like sarcasm do not come across well over unsolicited correspondence, simply because an agent cannot read your tone or see your expression.
- Personalize your query to each agent or market. No mass submissions to multiple people at the same time. Make sure that you have the agent's name spelled correctly. If the agent's name is "Sam Johnson" and you are not positive of the agent's gender, use neither "Mr. Johnson" nor "Mrs. Johnson." Just address the agent as "Sam Johnson."
- Make sure you fully understand the guidelines and are submitting the correct materials—if you're unsure, do more research.
- Make the e-mail's subject line exactly what the agent requests. If she doesn't specify, simply writing, "Query: (TITLE)" is a safe bet.
- Keep your emotions in check: Resist the temptation to send a response after being rejected such as "Please reconsider!" Keep your e-mails businesslike—and spend your time more effectively.
- Whether it's a print or e-mail submission, don't type in all caps or all lowercase. Use proper punctuation, and always pay attention to grammar and spelling.
- Double-check the mailing address or e-mail address. One wrong letter in an e-mail address is enough to lose your letter in cyberspace forever.
- If querying by e-mail, make sure all your font and type size is the same. Since you will be cutting and pasting into e-mail, different sentences can appear different sizes. Send yourself or a friend a test e-mail to check for such an issue.
- Make no demands. Anything that seems like a demand ("Respond to my letter within two weeks to respect my time") is a

major turnoff. Even polite requests can be annoying. It's not an agent's job to critique the work for you, so don't say, "I welcome feedback on my query letter and novel."

- Act with humility. No matter your current accomplishments, and no matter how much you think your novel is the best thing since *Breaking Bad*, you need to stay professional and simply discuss the story. Even if your writing history is impressive, be sure to state your accomplishments quickly and humbly.
- Keep a detailed list of submission information—such as where you sent queries and when or if you should personally hear back. This will prevent you from following up with agents too soon or nudging people who have specifically said, "If you don't hear from us, consider that a no. Do not follow up."
- Unless you have a serious health concern that prevents you from using a computer, submit your book yourself. Don't have a friend or relative submit your book for you. This kind of communication gets confusing, and the agent may not know who to address in correspondence. Plus, it can give an agent pause to wonder why the writer is not confident enough or able to submit his own work.
- Keep exclamation points, bold, underlined text, and italics to a minimum.
- Never submit any material for publication that you do not own the complete rights to. For example, don't submit a fan fiction novel about Batman or other copyrighted characters.
- Don't call. Yes, there will always be that one story of that one guy who called up an agency cold and got an agent on the phone and explained his story and the book became a bestseller. But reps have submission guidelines for a reason. Agents *hate* phone queries.
- If you do use snail mail, don't try to set yourself apart by using fancy stationery. Standard letterhead and envelopes are preferable.

"It's not necessary to formally copyright your work before submitting. Once you write it, legally the copyright is yours, so it looks amateurish to include the © mark on a manuscript. You can trust that agents and editors have no interest in stealing your unpublished work. What we really want is to work with you to get your manuscript published and then cheer you on as you write another one."

—Linda Epstein (Jennifer De Chiara Literary)

CONSIDERING REQUESTS FOR EXCLUSIVES

An exclusive submission is when an agent asks to be the only one reviewing your material at the current time. While virtually no agents ask for an exclusive query letter, this subject does start popping up when an agent requests your full manuscript. Some agents do not believe in this practice.

Agents who favor exclusives do so to protect their time: They don't want to spend their entire weekend reading a long novel, only to call the writer on Monday morning to offer representation and learn the author just signed with someone else last week. Typically these agents will reply to your query like this: "Thanks for your submission. The novel sounds intriguing. Please send me the full manuscript attached in a Word doc. I request an exclusive on the work for forty-five days."

At that point, it's up to you to decide whether or not to grant the agent the exclusive she asks for. Don't worry if the manuscript is already under review elsewhere; you can reply and explain just that.

> Dear Agent,
> Thank for you for your enthusiasm about [*Book Title*]. Attached, as requested, is the full manuscript, complete at [XX,000] words. Regarding your note about an exclusive, I must tell you that this full manuscript is already being reviewed by [x] other agents That said, I will honor your request for an exclusive by refrain-

ing from passing it out to any more agents for the next forty-five days. Thank you!

If you simply tell the truth and explain the situation, you have the best of all worlds. You, in a way, honor the agent's request. But you still have multiple agents considering the manuscript, and this latest agent gets to hear you say there is already enough interest in the book that other reps are hovering around it.

But let's be honest. Writers rarely get excited when an agent mentions an exclusive. It's exciting to see your work generate interest, but an exclusive can stop the submission process in its tracks. If a second agent were to write next week and ask to see the manuscript, you would have to tell her that the manuscript is under exclusive currently and that you can only pass it to her once the time frame expires in [X] days. This can be frustrating.

So here's a better way to go about it: If an agent asks for an exclusive, note that you can always send the manuscript (or nonfiction book proposal) to her and nicely decline her request for an exclusive review period. How she reacts to this decision is uncertain and could mean less interest or priority given to it, or it could mean no change whatsoever. Or you can limit the length of time for exclusives. If an agent asks for a "three-month exclusive on the full manuscript," you can respond with the manuscript and say that you would be happy to grant her an exclusive but wish to limit the time frame to one month (or six weeks or whatever you feel comfortable with). Lastly, if an agent asks for an exclusive and you agree to one—only to realize that no time frame was ever discussed— follow up after thirty days if you've received no note from the agent and politely ask her how much more time she thinks she requires.

PROTECT YOURSELF FROM SCAMMERS

From time to time, the submission waters can get a little murky—with scamming "agents" lurking in Internet shadows. Luckily this is not much of a concern nowadays as the job of the agent has evolved and become more standardized and search engines do a good job of keeping scammers from the top of the search results. But just to be safe, let's discuss how to protect yourself from unscrupulous people looking to make your wallet a little lighter.

The concept of literary scammers is nothing new and has evolved over time. Twenty years ago, some writers were still confused about whether agents were allowed to charge money simply to read your work and consider the project. So much confusion existed that databases divided agents into two categories: "fee-charging agents" and "non-fee-charging agents." Now you'd think that writers would have an easy time deciding who to contact, but plenty of agents who charged fees were skilled at selling books to editors, so a writer's query process was complicated.

Now fee-charging agents have been essentially eliminated from the mainstream marketplace. Today it's standard practice that an agent will never charge a writer any amount of money to review his work or represent his books. An agent should only make money when *you* make money. All agents are different, sure—with different personalities and skill levels and experience—but the biggest thing to watch out for is that agents do not charge you money up front.

"Watch for red flags. Reputable agents generally don't charge reading fees or require other up-front payments, they don't sell (or at least, don't brag about sales) to vanity presses, and they will readily identify other authors and projects they've represented."

—Howard Zaharoff, copyright and publishing lawyer

While today's pool of literary agents won't have a "fee-charging" category, the new danger to watch out for is false agencies on the Internet. Some scammers got wise to the Web years ago and realized that people who were uneducated in the publishing world were relying on Google too much and simply searching for "literary agency" online. This led to the creation of fake agencies.

These supposed agencies work like this: After you submit, the agency sends you a form letter saying that they read your novel and love the writing. They offer you representation, and you agree, even signing a letter of consent. Then, once you're hooked, they say the book needs some work. This is where the euphemisms come into play. It's never a "fee"; it's always something like a "marketing investment" or an "editorial review." You fear you're already in too deep to stop now, and you fork over the money and hope for the best. But the fake agency never provides any worthwhile edits, and they pocket the money. And whether the agency edits it or not, they have no true ability to sell the book, because they're not a legitimate establishment and have no real connections. Bingo— you've been scammed.

But like I said, writers today are generally savvy to the submission process, and the mere fact that you're reading this book makes me think you have nothing to worry about. All you have to do to protect yourself is two simple things.

1. **USE TRUSTWORTHY DATABASES THAT SCREEN FOR ANY QUES- TIONABLE AGENCIES.** In addition to the *Guide to Literary Agents*, I suggest Querytracker.com and Publishersmarketplace.com. Stick with the documented professionals, and you will steer clear of any worry. While not every rep has a charming personality or the IQ needed for MENSA admission, I do assure you that legit agents will not rip you off and will not steal your work—and that's what's important.

2. **RESEARCH, RESEARCH, RESEARCH.** When in doubt, *research*. Before you submit to an agency, look for interviews with their agents. Investigate them on Facebook and Twitter. See what books they've represented. Believe me: If the writing public has concerns about an agency, the Internet will tell you very quickly. You see, writers are a thoughtful, intelligent bunch—but they're

also vindictive. And if an agency online is scamming people, writers will swarm over to message boards and forums like piranhas to sound the alarm. That means if XYZ Agency is not a legit choice, all you would have to do is Google "XYZ Agency"— some of the top results would be warnings not to submit to them.

If you ever have a strange gut feeling about dealing with someone, feel free to check out the following popular watchdog sites that alert writers about deceitful individuals.

- **WRITER BEWARE:** www.sfwa.org/other-resources/for-authors/writer-beware
- **PREDITORS & EDITORS:** Pred-ed.com

Both of these sites were created to protect writers from scammers. Use them on your journey.

BEWARE OF EDITING SERVICE REFERRALS

If you do your homework and only use trusted databases of agents (whether in print or online), your likelihood of running into a scammer is virtually nil. Furthermore, now that you've read this chapter, you'll recognize the warning signs should you come across the website of an unknown, untrusted agency. But there is one more thing that you should be aware of: *editing service referrals*. This problem is rare, but it happens.

It works like this. An agent rejects your submission and says that the book needs more work or that it needs an editorial eye. She then suggests a specific editing service or individual who can help. The problem here is that the agent may be getting a kickback from the editor for each successful referral, and that's bad. The only times I've ever felt comfortable with agents referring writers to editing services is when they suggest several to choose from and openly state that they receive no financial compensation in the matter. Sometimes, on their websites, agents will refer writers to editing services run by their clients. As long as the agent is forthright that (1) yes, these are her clients' services, as she's trying to help them, and (2) she gets no kickbacks whatsoever, it's okay to check out her suggestions. If you're leery, simply look for editing services elsewhere.

GETTING TO KNOW THE AAR

Did you ever personally think about becoming an agent and representing writers? Well, guess what—all you have to do is snap your fingers, and it's done. I'm not kidding. There is no exam or degree. All you or I or anyone has to do is simply print up some business cards, build a website, and put out a call for queries. That's it.

This may sound like a shaky proposition, but that's where the Association of Authors' Representatives (AAR) comes in. The AAR is the closest thing to an accreditation body for an agent, and it exists as a verification organization for representatives. The following statement can be found on the AAR website: "Authors can be confident that our agents pledge to follow the highest standards of professional conduct in serving the needs of their clients."

To be accepted into the AAR means meeting certain criteria set forth by the group: An agent "must have at least two years as a full-time working agent, with at least ten reportable sales over an eighteen-month period, and be primarily responsible for executing publishing agreements, translation or performance rights in these properties. Applications need to be accompanied by two letters of reference from current members." The AAR also accepts representations at an "associate agent" level, which is a tier below established agents. To be in this second tier, an agent "must be currently employed at an agency and should demonstrate an increasing level of responsibility. Applications need to be accompanied by a letter of reference from a full member at your current agency."

The AAR has more than four hundred member agents—most are book agents, but some are dramatic agents dealing with theater.

If you see the letters AAR by the name of an agent, you can feel secure that she's a tried-and-true rep with a history of sales and is dedicated to treating clients with top professionalism.

But what does this imply regarding non-AAR personnel? Can those agents be trusted? My answer is: In all likelihood, *yes*.

The AAR has four hundred agents in the organization, but there are one thousand–plus agents nationwide. So taking a strict view of the matter (such as "I need an AAR agent or bust") is not the wisest approach. I can speak from experience: My agent, Sorche Fairbank of Fairbank Literary Representation, was not part of the AAR when I signed with her in 2008, though she joined the organization years later. If I would have turned down her offer of representation simply because she lacked three initials after her name, we wouldn't have sold any of our six books together.

If you're concerned about protecting yourself and your work during the query process, remember to research and look for key elements: what the agent did before agenting, if she is part of a larger agency, if she has sold any books to publishers, and if there are complaints against her online concerning any kind of fees or work practices. The initials after a name are great to consider but should not be the absolute, deciding factor.

NOTE: *You can read the entire AAR Canon of Ethics in this book's resources section.*

GETTING AN AGENT FOR

YOUR SELF-PUBLISHED BOOK

What I want to do in this chapter is not spell out *how* to self-publish your book but rather *how to pitch* an existing self-published work to literary agents. Doing so is a different proposition than pitching an unpublished "new" manuscript. This topic is especially relevant in today's marketplace, as the ease of self-publishing and e-publishing has made such a path more reputable and much more common.

When you contact agents to pitch a self-published book, you must disclose that the work in question is indeed previously published, as well as through what channels it is currently available and how long it's been out. You do not have to mention any previous self-published books that have nothing to do with what you're pitching (though you certainly may include mentions if sales are good).

A self-published book is any book where the decision to publish the book was the author's alone and/or the transaction involved the author paying any up-front costs for services. This includes:

- E-publishing—such as Smashwords and CreateSpace
- Vanity presses
- Print-on-Demand (P.O.D.) publishers
- Book printers

Basically, if you think your book falls under the umbrella of "self-published" books, then it almost certainly does, and that means you must pitch it as one.

HOW TO PITCH A SELF-PUBLISHED BOOK

Pitching a self-published book to a literary agent is a tougher road to submission than other roads. That's because when agents review a query for an unpublished novel, they're looking for voice and story. When agents review a query for a self-published novel, they're looking for voice and story—and they're *also* looking for one or several good reasons why this book deserves a second life via traditional publishing. So give them those good reasons!

Agents look for factors that hint at money and success. You are trying to show that your book is head and shoulders above the other million items that are self-published each year and thus demands fresh attention. So here are four elements to include in a query letter for your self-published book that can impress an agent.

1. **SALES NUMBERS.** How many copies has the book sold? And by *sold*, I don't mean free downloads. How many print books have you sold? How many e-books? (And since it's assumed e-books are usually downloaded at $0.99, have wording in your query if the price was higher). "Impressive" sales numbers differ from agent to agent, but you shouldn't query before you've sold at least two to three thousand print books or between ten thousand and twenty thousand e-books.
2. **AWARDS AND ANY RECOGNITION.** Did your book make any online "best of" lists? Did it reach number one in any category

bestseller lists on Amazon? Has it collected any accolades that vouch for its content and quality? Such recognition could be a local honor, a niche fiction award, or anything else. Most books do not gain accolades, so having one attached to your book can make an agent sit up and take notice.

3. **HIGH-PROFILE ENDORSEMENTS OR BLURBS.** Since your book's release, has it attracted the attention of any notable authors, politicians, celebrities, or persons of interest? If so, whom? What did they say about the book? Have you personally asked them if you can use the endorsement as a book blurb on the cover of future print copies? A blurb from a recognizable name is a great marketing tool, and agents know this.

4. **MEDIA ATTENTION OR REVIEWS.** Has your book received a review in any mainstream publications or media outlets, such as morning TV shows (local or otherwise), newspapers, magazines, or notable blogs? If so, explain some of the greatest hits. Obviously, the bigger the better. Please keep in mind that Amazon reviews do not count. Meanwhile, if you're donating a portion of the book's proceeds to charity, and thus the charity is promoting your book for you, that, too, would be something to mention in the query because it equals sales and money.

WILL AN AGENT FIND YOUR SELF-PUBLISHED BOOK AND CONTACT YOU?

Many authors hope that, after a book is self-published and available for purchase, a literary agent will come across the work and come calling. Does this happen? Occasionally. Does this happen with any degree of regularity? Absolutely not.

Some agents make an effort to scan Amazon's e-book bestseller lists and find hidden gems that are blowing up the charts.

In fact, this happened to Colleen Houck, author of *Tiger's Curse*. After she e-published her book and spread the word to friends, it remarkably made its way to the number one spot on the Kindle children's bestseller lists for seven straight weeks. Getting to that spot for just one week would have been impressive, but seven straight weeks is quite amazing. This feat attracted attention from all kinds of places. Says Houck: "Costco contacted me about selling my series in some of their stores. I was contacted by China, Thailand, and Korea to see if the translation rights had been sold. A film producer e-mailed me. My world was spinning when a literary agent contacted me. He said he'd found me on Amazon and was impressed with my reviews. Two days later I had representation at one of the top, if not the best, agency in the country, Trident Media Group. My new agent went to work immediately. Within a few weeks, I had a [traditional] book deal."

So this possible path to an agent can indeed happen, but it's a rarity in a marketplace glutted with self-published works. That's why, rather than waiting for an agent to swoop in from out of nowhere and take control of your career, you should take one of three other routes with your book instead.

1. **TRY FOR AN AGENT *FIRST*.** Since you're reading this book, I'm guessing this has been your plan all along. I urge you not to self-publish the book outright without trying to get an agent. Instead, try the traditional publishing route and give your novel a fair chance. Remember that it's easier to get an agent to represent a book that is not already available online.

2. **GATHER AMMUNITION AND ACCOLADES FOR YOUR QUERY LETTER.** If you do self-publish, you cannot count on agents finding you. You'll have to query them yourself, and, as discussed previously, your query letter has to give them a reason to be interested in your writing. So actively collect media attention, endorsements, awards, and more for your book. These items don't come quickly or easily, but including them in your query letter will immediately make your work stand out among other self-published books.

3. **SIMPLY LET THE BOOK(S) REMAIN SELF-PUBLISHED.** Here's a hard truth: While there are plenty of quality self-published books produced every year, most aren't traditionally published for a reason. Only the crème de la crème of novels and nonfiction books are published through traditional houses and see the inside of bookstores. Remember that, as writers, we get more skilled over time—bettering our craft with each novel, book, and short story we write. So it's perfectly acceptable to simply let the book remain self-published and move on. In other words, write a new novel and then query for *that* manuscript.

LITERARY AGENT ROUNDUP
READING PITCHES FOR SELF-PUBLISHED BOOKS

"I am open to self-published books, but I find the time it takes to evaluate them is often better spent on books that haven't been published. Oftentimes a self-published author will just send a link for me to look at, which I never click, or they send the book in a Word doc or PDF for me to evaluate. In addition, authors aren't immediately transparent on sales or download info. I find self-published authors make me work too hard for the information I need. For self-published authors to get my attention, I need transparency around sales and download figures and want a straightforward and professional query without buy links or embedded images. Don't make me work to get the information."

—Elizabeth Kracht (Kimberley Cameron & Associates)

"My thoughts for self-pub are similar to any type of query as far as the pitch itself. It should be clear, concise, compelling (we'll call it the three Cs!), and well written. As far as the self-pub background, I need to know the realities of the publication

history, even if that means it's only sold three hundred copies in four months. Frankly, if the sales are low, I'd prefer to see a pitch for a new book—and not one that's part of a series from the first one."

—Stacey Glick (Dystel & Goderich)

"The good news: The stigma of vanity publishing and self-published books not being good enough has been proven false by the 'Kindle Millionaires' and other self-published authors who are making a comfortable living going it alone. The bad news: The expectations of a self-published author are higher than they've ever been, both in sales numbers and in social media marketing muscle. When I receive a query from someone who has self-published a book, I want to know how many books you've sold yourself, how extensive is your social media presence (I will Google you!), and what your future plans are. If you've published the first book in a series, don't pitch me the second, because zero publishers will be interested in publishing your sequel if they don't have the first book. And don't tell me that you're looking for an agent because you haven't sold very many self-published books and you want a publisher to help you accomplish that. They are going to run into the same obstacles you are. When you're looking for an agent, you might mention that you self-published prior to now, but pitch me on an unpublished book that I can sell to a traditional publisher."

—Laurie McLean (Fuse Literary)

PART TWO

YOUR SUBMISSION TOOLS

CHAPTER SIX

THE ALL-IMPORTANT

QUERY LETTER

A query letter is a one-page letter that serves as your first contact with agents. In it you will spell out what your novel or nonfiction book is about and who you are. On the strength of this letter and its effectiveness, agents will decide if they want to learn more about your book and read its first few chapters.

The value of a good query cannot be ignored. Sure, there are some agents out there who blow by the letter and want to see your sample pages, but the majority of agents still place a lot of value on this first contact and pitch. Some authors have even described the process of whittling a complete book down to several sentences as more difficult than writing the book itself.

You may be asking, "But why send them a short letter about my work? Why not just send them the novel or memoir so they can judge the content by its true merit? Why add this extra, strange step?" The simple answer is that a literary agent is incredibly busy and overworked. If she accepted entire manuscripts upon initial contact, the manuscripts would quickly pile up to the ceiling and block the doorway. The query letter is part of a filtering system. It keeps the slush pile from getting out of control and, more important, helps agents decide whether a manuscript is worth reviewing or not.

Thus the query letter reigns—and that's the key.

But fear not. In this chapter—and the next chapter, which provides successful examples—we will break down the query letter from head to toe. While there are many ways to write a query, I can tell you that, after critiquing almost one thousand of these letters over the years, there is definitely a tried-and-true formula that stands above the rest. It's a four-part approach that includes a simple introduction, an effective pitch, a writer bio, and contact information. Throughout this chapter, we'll explore each section, how to write it, and why it's a vital part of your query. We'll look first at fiction before moving on to additional insights for nonfiction authors.

QUERY LETTER FORMATTING: QUICK TIPS

- The generally advised length is one Microsoft Word page, single-spaced. The only time you may need to go over one page in length is if you're pitching nonfiction and your platform and marketing information runs long.
- Use block formatting. This means that text is pushed left and there is a blank line between paragraphs.
- Include a date at the top of the letter, and push it right.
- Like your manuscript, use 12-point font. And while any standard, default font will likely be satisfactory, Times New Roman is still the gold standard.
- If querying by e-mail (which you will do 90 percent of the time), put your contact information—phone, blog, Twitter handle, etc.—at the bottom of the letter, under your signature, not at the top.

LITERARY AGENT ROUNDUP
QUERY LETTER BASICS

"Queries are business letters. Agenting is business. Publishing is business. I try to be nice and friendly and funny and all, but the bottom line is that I expect those with whom I work to be professional and take what they're doing seriously."

—Linda Epstein (Jennifer De Chiara Literary)

"The best query letters convey the tone of the book."

—Mollie Glick (Foundry Literary + Media)

"I dislike it when a query letter focuses too much on the author's bio and doesn't tell me what the book is about. Make sure you include essential story details."

—Shira Hoffman (McIntosh & Otis, Inc.)

"First, take heart—agents really will read a great query. For queries, here's a secret: Any agent will read a well-researched, personal query. Show the agent that you know a little about the list that she pours so much time and care into. You can do this by stating something such as, 'I'm writing to you because I loved Book X and I know that you represent Writer Z.' Then write a smart, focused query."

—Lindsay Edgecombe (Levine Greenberg Rostan Literary Agency)

"I'm sure it has been said before, but the best queries are the ones that are pitched to agents who share your sensibilities. Don't pitch an agent who specializes in science fiction a book about financial markets and vice versa. Also, avoid the term fiction novel."

—Melissa Flashman (Trident Media Group)

"I love a query that reads like the back of a book cover. Also, I do encourage all writers to treat their query as a job interview. Be professional. Be concise."

—Nicole Resciniti (The Seymour Agency)

"Spell-check your letter. Follow all the agent's directions for submitting a query."

—Dawn Dowdle (Blue Ridge Literary Agency)

"Being able to really articulate what you want to say in a short query is difficult yet extremely important. We need to see something that jumps out at us as different, passionate, and expressive. On a daily basis, our team reads and considers several submissions, so it is those ideas that promise change and innovation that catch our eye."

—Jan Miller (Dupree/Miller & Associates)

"The silliest mistake I see in a submission (and I see it surprisingly often) is an unprofessional query letter. I've received queries for 'Dear Editor,' 'Dear Agent,' 'Dear Publisher,' as well as e-mail queries that are addressed to ten different agents together. I wonder if people really think someone will want to work with you if you can't be bothered to get their name right. A little homework and a professional letter that provides all the information we request in our submissions guidelines on our website is the best way to showcase your work and send the message that you will be pleasant to work with."

—Jacqueline Flynn (Joelle Delbourgo Associates)

"Query letters do need a voice. Some voice. Your voice. You can tell when a writer is a natural and can convey simple ideas and plot summary without being boring or giving away too much."

—Elana Roth (Red Tree Literary)

"Avoid a sentence such as 'This is my third (or fourth, or fifth, or sixth) unpublished novel, so I am clearly very dedicated and hardworking ...'"

—Alex Glass (Trident Media Group)

"Watch those typos, folks! We do notice."

—Peter McGuigan (Foundry Literary + Media)

"Ever since I started taking electronic submissions, I've found that many people don't put the care into query letters that they would have in a hardcopy submission. It's as if they see an electronic query letter more as another random e-mail than a professional introduction to their work. So I'm seeing the disturbing, 'Hey, I've got this manuscript I think is right up your alley. Can I send it?' sort of letters. Writers should think of the query as they would a cover letter that goes along with a résumé. You wouldn't dash that off carelessly (or CC it to everyone in the field, another common mistake), so don't do it with query letters."

—Lucienne Diver (The Knight Agency)

FICTION QUERY LETTER, SECTION 1: THE INTRO

A safe and simple way to start your letter is with a quick introductory paragraph. This is one of the easiest query elements to compose, and your goal is to begin and end it as quickly as possible. The intro is the same for both fiction and nonfiction submissions.

The intent of this opening paragraph is twofold. First, you want to quickly introduce the crucial details of the work—specifically the genre, title, word count, and fact that it is completed. Examples follow.

> BEWARE THE TRUTH is a completed 89,000-word techno-thriller.

Or:

> I am seeking representation for MRS. MADELINE MUFFINS,
> a completed picture book of approximately 700 words, which
> has been professionally illustrated.

Secondly, this intro paragraph gives you an easy chance to establish a connection with an agent. After all, if there are thirteen hundred practicing literary agents in the country, a quick sentence can illuminate why are you reaching out to this particular one. Agents like to feel a deep connection to a project and often enjoy it when a writer chooses them for a good reason. The good news for writers is that creating this "connection sentence" is not difficult. There are three very easy ways to do it.

1. **MENTION A WRITERS CONFERENCE CONNECTION.** If you met the agent at a writers conference, say so, especially if you pitched your book to her there. It cuts through the smoke and immediately shows that you two have met before and that you're a professional writer who is taking the task of improving your craft seriously.

   > I saw you speak at the 2014 Writer's Digest Conference
   > and loved your advice on how to create compelling fiction.

2. **CITE THE AGENT'S PAST BOOK SALES.** Perhaps you're contacting the agent specifically because of the type(s) of books she's sold in the past. If so, explain just that.

   > Because you represented previous hard science fiction
   > books such as *The Neptune Paradox* and *Ultra-Sphere*, I
   > think you might also enjoy my sci-fi novel, *Light Speed*.

3. **REFERENCE SOMETHING THE AGENT SAID IN AN INTERVIEW OR ONLINE.** She'll reveal all kinds of interesting tidbits and preferences through blog interviews and Twitter, which you can then use in your query.

> I saw in your interview on the *Guide to Literary Agents* blog that you're actively seeking contemporary middle-grade fiction for boys ...

Or:

> Because you put a call out on Twitter for more stories with animal protagonists, I thought you might like to take a look at my novel ...

Or:

> I saw on your agency website that you lived overseas in China for a year. I hope that my story—set in both America and China—will be of interest to you ...

HOW DO YOU IDENTIFY THE AGENT OF A PARTICULAR BOOK?

If an agent repped a successful book in your genre, she would likely be a good fit for your book, too. There are two easy ways this can typically be done.

1. **LOOK IN THE ACKNOWLEDGMENTS SECTION OF THE BOOK.** Almost every book—whether fiction or nonfiction—has an acknowledgments page where the author spills his gratitude. Ten times out of ten, her agent is listed here.
2. **SEARCH THE AUTHOR'S WEBSITE.** If you're looking for the agent of John Q. Writer, search the Internet for an official author website. Most of the time, such a website will exist. Then start looking around the website for the agent's name. Check the Contact page, if there is one, as the writer usually lists the information for his agent and publicist.

Even though the intro paragraph is simple and quick, you may wonder: Is it completely necessary? Is it possible to just jump right to the book and begin with a pitch? You can—and some writers certainly do just that—but I've found that there can be a problem with that approach that will sink your query: *confusion*. Don't perplex an agent with what you say, or they'll reject you.

To understand this better, imagine yourself as an agent who opens up a new e-query. The first line reads, "Billy has a problem, and life will never be the same after today." Here's the issue with such an opening line: Who *is* Billy? Is Billy a nine-year-old whose pet goldfish was just washed down the drain? Or is Billy a Special Forces officer who was just taken hostage outside of Pakistan? You can see how this causes immediate confusion about the tone and plot of the book. But if you had an introductory line saying that the work was middle-grade fiction or saying it was an international military thriller, the confusion disappears. Explaining the details up front helps the agent quickly wrap her head around what is to come.

Some agents and writers advise starting the query with a "hook line"— a quick, intriguing sentence. This tactic can indeed work, but, in my opinion, most lines fall flat and therefore work against you. Writers sometimes take this advice to mean starting with a rhetorical question, such as:

What would you do if it were your last day on Earth?

But here's the rub: Agents (like many readers) generally dislike rhetorical questions because they are all similar to one another, and they are, by definition, questions that are not supposed to be answered.

Meanwhile, starting off with a quick, two-sentence "safe" intro paragraph is a successful and simple means to get the ball rolling and connect with an agent. Even if an agent states online that she tends to enjoy something like a "hook line," virtually no one will reject you outright if you take the safe route and start with a quick intro paragraph.

FICTION QUERY LETTER, SECTION 2: THE PITCH

Once the intro's come and gone, it's time to get into the most important part of the query letter: *the pitch*—a brief basic description of your novel or memoir designed to pique the agent's interest. For fiction writers, this will be the longest and most difficult section to compose. It's tough to boil down an entire book into a few condensed paragraphs, but I've developed a six-step formula for how to lay out a pitch for any fictional story.

General Pitch Tips

But first, let's start with a broad approach. Since everyone is writing a different tale with different characters, no two pitches will be alike, but there are seven qualities that unite all pitches.

- **PITCHES ARE THREE TO TEN SENTENCES.** Conciseness is a very good thing. If you write more than ten sentences, your letter runs the risk of going over one page and also simply rambling.

- **PITCHES DO NOT REVEAL THE ENDING.** If, when describing my latest novel, I told you that the good guy wins in the end but his girl dies and the bomb sets it up for a sequel … would you still want to read the book? Probably not. If you're like most people, you don't *want* to know how the story ends, so retain the intrigue and suspense.

- **PITCHES ARE COMPARABLE TO COPY ON DVD BOXES AND THE BACK COVERS OF NOVELS.** If you're having trouble putting together a pitch, visit your nearest Barnes & Noble or Target, or any other place that sells both books and movies. Pick up both films and books in your genre (e.g., children's stories, Christian fiction, etc.), and start reading the boxes, back covers, and jackets. Those are all pitch examples for you to study and emulate. See what grabs your attention, and copy that strategy.

- **BE SPECIFIC, AND AVOID GENERALITIES.** Specific elements bring a pitch to life, and generalities drag it down. Don't say, "The couple goes through many highs and lows"; explain what that means, exactly, even if you're just touching on a bigger picture. "Avoid vagueness," says Bridget Smith of Dunham Literary. "I get so many queries every day that don't tell me enough about the novel. If there's no reason for me to say yes, then it's going to be no." Being specific paints pictures in the reader's mind. If I tell you that my main character "just quit his job," does that create an image in your mind? Probably not. But how about if I told you, "After making his thousandth Big Mac, seventeen-year-old Rodney Morrison makes a spontaneous decision to quit his job in style—by launching a cupful of special sauce out the drive-through window at a rude customer before walking out the front door with his middle fingers in the air." Now, does *that* paint a picture in your mind? Yes.

- **AIM TO ELICIT EMOTION.** The style and voice of the pitch itself should reflect the book's contents. Don't say, "My novel is a humorous romp with quirky characters." The agent is giving you three to ten sentences to make her laugh. Can you do that? Don't say, "My novel is full of suspenseful twists and turns." Rather than talk about your novel from a distance, the agent is giving you three to ten sentences to put a chill down her spine. If you're writing light, humorous women's fiction, then you should include some laughs in the query letter. If you're writing a dark horror novel, then you should include some spooky elements. Imagine you read the line: "But as Candace continues to explore the world of erotic asphyxiation, she becomes addicted to the feeling and even begins to choke herself on lunch breaks just to experience the sensation." Such a line hits you and can make you feel repulsed, intrigued, or engaged. It triggers your emotions. If you can appeal to an agent's emotions, she's much more inclined to request more material—because you've *shown* her that your writing connects to readers rather than just *told* her.

- **BEWARE OF SUBPLOTS AND UNNECESSARY DETAILS.** Pitches often go too long because they're bogged down with superfluous elements. A simple way to avoid this is to cut out the small stuff:

Leave plot elements, setting description, and proper nouns on the cutting-room floor. For example, look at these two potential beginnings of a pitch.

VERSION 1: Zalisa is a teenage elven princess who lives on a jungle planet. Despite her desire to live a common life welding swords, she is repeatedly told by her parents about her destiny to become queen and bring peace between warring tribes as their supreme leader. (Word count: 46, two sentences)

VERSION 2: Zalisa, part of the chosen Y'Ri noble elves, lives with the Sha'NaRee tribe on the jungle planet of Usulurah. Adorned with long hair down to her waist and many tattoos she's designed herself, all Zalisa wants is a life among the commoners doing what she loves best: sword making. She has quietly developed an amazing knack for intricate blade making and trained with the highest levels of metalworkers and smiths in her province of Va'Quenay. The only problem is that her parents, E'Leepha and Can-Yur, expect their daughter to refrain from frolicking among the commoners and instead fulfill the destiny of Tritonalt, a great prophecy widely known to all citizens of Usulurah. According to Tritonalt, Zalisa is the chosen royal descendent who will ascend to the throne as part of a divine prediction foretold by the ancient elven wise men at the 7 Cycles of Wisdom gathering eons ago when all the system's planets were in line with the sun. Once she has ascended to the throne, it is foretold that Zalisa will quell the constant warfare that has hampered the planet and finally bring peace to the land. (Word count: 186, six sentences.)

The second intro is chock-full of stuff we don't need to know right now: the proper names of things (such as the planet name), her exact appearance outside of being an elf (e.g., the tattoos), and the backstory about how the prophecy came to be (the gathering). The second version has already used up most of the query page—six pitch sentences out of a maximum ten—and there's no discussion of what happens throughout the meat of the plot, what challenges Zalisa faces, or what she sets off to do to overcome said challenges.

- **PRACTICE, AND HAVE DIFFERENT VERSIONS IF NEED BE.** Tell your pitch to others, or get your query formally critiqued by a professional or peers. If you can't decide between two versions of a pitch, you can always try out both and keep tabs on which agents get which versions. If one is garnering better responses than the other, you have your answer concerning how best to move forward.

HOW TO SUBMIT ILLUSTRATIONS, IMAGES, OR ARTICLE CLIPS

Most agents request that you do not send attachments with your e-query. They want pasted text only when you first contact them. And yes, that does mean pasting your entire query, synopsis, and first chapters right into the body of an e-mail. But some agents do want attachments—especially if you're submitting art such as illustrations or photos for consideration.

If you want to submit art but the agent says no attachments, it's best to share a link that takes her to a website where she can view your images. Place this link at the end of your letter. If you have photos for the book, you can post them on Flickr or Photobucket whenever you like and just link to the album in your query. Perhaps you could post some of your illustrations on your website as well. This is a safe way to share art with an agent without getting your query deleted because of unwanted attachments.

The Seven Parts to Any Fiction or Memoir Pitch

1. **INTRODUCE THE MAIN CHARACTER(S).** Remember that agents review a large number of pitches each week and that doing so can be overwhelming. Getting them attached to your character right away keeps them interested in your pitch. If you have two equal main characters (e.g., Bill and Ted, Laverne and Shirley), you should show them both at the beginning. One totally accept-

able exception to *not* starting with your main character is if you need a single line defining something we absolutely need to know, such as "In the near future, class systems of humans emerge based on zodiac signs" or "1850s London: The entire population lives in fear of the plague." If you do use an establishing sentence this way, make sure it's absolutely necessary and cannot be incorporated after the introduction of the main character(s).

2. **TELL US SOMETHING ABOUT THIS MAIN CHARACTER—AN IN-TERESTING TIDBIT (2A), WHAT HE WANTS (2B), OR BOTH.** After you've done the quick task of telling the agents who your main character is, you must get them to have a vested interest in that character. So tell them a noteworthy attribute of the character, explain what he desires in life, or both.

> **PITCH IN PROGRESS (PARTS 1, 2A, 2B)**
>
> FINDING NEMO is a story about Marlin, a clownfish (1) who worries about practically everything. If he had his way, he'd never risk leaving the sea anemone he calls home (2a). The one thing he wants more than anything in life is to guide and protect his son (2b), Nemo—because Marlin knows what a dangerous place the ocean is and Nemo is the only family he has.

3. **REVEAL THE INCITING INCIDENT.** The inciting incident is the event that sets the story in motion. It is usually easy to spot in a story because it happens early in the book and without it, you wouldn't have a novel. This can be a person dying, a crime being committed, or someone getting fired—the action in the plot that changes the main character's life and forces him to act and grow.

4. **LAY OUT THE MAIN CONFLICT OR PLOT OF THE STORY.** After you've explained what goes wrong (the inciting incident), explain the character's response—what he sets out to do. When you write this sentence, you should essentially be spelling out the main plot and arc of the story.

PITCH IN PROGRESS (PARTS 3, 4)

But overprotective Marlin can't stay in the sea anemone for long. His worst fears come true when Nemo is captured by human scuba divers and taken away in a speedboat (3). Now Marlin must make the long, dangerous swim to the Australian coast so he can rescue his son (4)—and the only help he'll have is from an overly friendly fish named Dory who (humorously) suffers from short-term memory loss.

5. **LIST SOME COMPLICATIONS.** Stories always get more complicated before conflicts resolve. So after you explain what the main character sets off to do (i.e., the main plot), tell the agent what goes wrong along the way. If you're writing an international spy novel, this is where you mention that the journey takes the hero to Switzerland, then Russia, and then back to America. If you're writing a humorous, lighthearted story, this is where you introduce some comic mishaps and supporting characters.

6. **CONCLUDE WITH AN OPEN-ENDED WRAP-UP.** Finish the query without explaining the climax or how it all wraps up at the end. Resist the urge, once again, to use a rhetorical question, such as "Will she find the bomb in time?"

7. **INCLUDE THE STAKES.** The agent needs to know what happens if the main character fails to complete his task: Does the world end? Does the love of his life move away forever? The thing that makes this part of the pitch unusual is that the stakes can show up anywhere in the pitch, whereas parts 1 through 6 typically go in that order (though that, too, is not completely mandatory).

PITCH IN PROGRESS (PARTS 5, 6, 7)

While little Nemo gets used to his new home (a small aquarium in a dentist's office), his former worrywart of a father now faces all the dangers that the ocean has to offer (5): dangerous sharks, crazy creatures at the bottom of the ocean, an army of jellyfish—all the while inching closer to the Australian coast and his lost boy. But when little Nemo becomes the next fish in line to be adopted and taken from the aquarium forever (7), Marlin's time to find his son is quickly running out (6).

Complete Pitch Samples

Now that you've seen a pitch broken down piece by piece, let's examine two more pitches and see how they differ and why those differences are important. Note how the good pitch examples have all aforementioned seven parts of the pitch nicely laid out, whereas the poor pitch examples do not.

Bad Pitch Example 1 (Fiction)

My novel, *To the Edge,* pits the skilled (a) Jake Miller up against a foe whose malice knows no bounds (b). When Jake has his world (c) shattered by this enemy, he sets off on a journey (d) to find the perpetrator and make things right (e). This odyssey tests his strength every day. Relying on his hopes, dreams, and unique skill sets (f), he is able to fight his way back into the light and finally confront his enemy. As Jake grapples with his new villain and fate itself, he discovers is much more to himself than he ever realized (g) and that he'll need it all if he is to survive. After all, how far will we go to save the ones we love (h)?

a) Skilled in *what?*
b) This is general and vague.
c) His world was never defined in the first place, so this beat has no value.
d) What kind of journey?
e) Unclear and vague
f) All of these are vague and undefined. They could mean anything.
g) More lackluster language and generalities

h) If at all possible, do not end (or begin) your pitch with a rhetorical question.

Good Pitch Example 1 (Fiction)

Daisy Arthur (a), alone since her husband of twenty-five years died yelling at golf on television (b), is retired, bored, and lonely (c). So she does what any sensible woman would do—joins a romance writers group (d). There are just a couple of problems with this plan. First, Daisy can't write so much as a shopping list to save her life (e). Second—and more pressing—one of her writing-group colleagues has just been found dead (f) in Colorado's Platte River (g). He's been murdered, and the rest of the writing group—including Daisy—are suspects, as they were the last ones to see him alive.

Daisy begins asking questions and looking into the murder (h), figuring that searching for the killer in her quirky writing bunch is a better option than becoming the group's next victim (i). And the good news is that her sleuthing gives her the chance to reconnect with old flame Gabe Capernilly, a single police lieutenant now in charge of the murder case (j). But while Daisy sees Gabe as a potential Mr. Right, Gabe sees her as the prime murder suspect (k).

a) The main character is immediately introduced (part 1).
b) Vivid specifics paint a picture in our minds. This beat also introduces humor.
c) Aspects of the main character (part 2a)
d) Illuminates what the main character desires—a new path in life and romance itself (part 2b)
e) Quick, effective humor
f) The inciting incident (part 3)
g) Simple way to introduce the setting
h) The main plot of the novel spelled out to us (part 4)
i) The stakes (part 7)

j) The complications (part 5), which also get us back to what the main character wants in life: a new romance

k) The final line ends with an unclear wrap-up (part 6).

Good Pitch Example 2 (Fiction)

> Sixteen-year-old Rosalie Clements (a) never dreamt of leaving civilized nineteenth-century Boston (b)—until her father dies (c), leaving her alone and destitute (d). But he has also willed her a clue that may lead to an elusive West Indian treasure. Desperate for money, Rosalie trades her skirts for breeches and heads for the Indies (e).
>
> But although she can soon raise a sail, brandish a cutlass, and lie as easily as she once drank tea (f), all is not smooth sailing (g). She has to evade much more than discovery on board: Her shipmates detest her incompetence, and the ship is a breeding ground for mutiny. Worse, after recovering from her shock at the rough life aboard, she soon becomes as intoxicated with her new life of adventure (h) as the other sailors are with daily grog rations. But when Rosalie discovers that Captain Beardslee (i), the most feared pirate of the Indies, and the crew aboard his aptly named ship, *The Cutthroat*, want the treasure, too, the race for the Indies becomes a race for survival (j).

a) The main character is introduced quickly (part 1), and since her age is important, it's revealed immediately.

b) The setting is unusual, so the writer wisely moves this info up front.

c) The inciting incident that propels Rosalie's journey into motion (part 3)

d) Explains what the main character wants (part 2b): a way out of desperation

e) The plot of the novel (part 4)

f) All of these are specifics—designed to paint mental pictures of her adventures.

g) Good wordplay, considering the plot

h) The character arc is apparent

i) A lot of this second paragraph reveals the plot complications (part 5), the most important of which is Beardslee.

j) Unclear, suspenseful wrap-up with the stakes mixed in (parts 6 and 7)

PITCHING A PICTURE BOOK

Pitching a children's picture book (ages four to eight) is an unusual task, as the pitch itself may run longer than the book's text. For this unique task, we consult literary agent Kelly Sonnack of Andrea Brown Literary Agency: "Include two to four sentences about your story that will pique the agent's interest. For examples of snappy recaps, study the publishers' descriptions of your favorites on Amazon or other retailers. A hook should still always be emphasized: 'A book about the love and support a child gets from her family, as shown with the two hands of each family member who helps her grow' (Diane Adams's *Two Hands to Love You*)."

FICTION QUERY LETTER, SECTION 3: THE BIO

The bio section of a query letter is a completely different beast for fiction and nonfiction. If you're writing nonfiction, the bio section is typically long and of the utmost importance: This is where you list all of your credentials as well as the greatest hits of your writer platform (more on that in chapter twelve). The importance of a nonfiction bio cannot be overstated. It has to be fat and awesome. Fiction bios, however, can be big or small or even nonexistent. Here I'll address fiction query bios—we'll look at nonfiction bio material later in the chapter.

Before you dig into these specifics, know that no matter what you are discussing—something notable (perhaps a past book that sold well) or something small (a local award)—always mention things quickly and humbly. Mention the point, and then back off. If you blabber on about an impressive accomplishment, it may come off as egotistical. If you yammer about something unimpressive, then it may look like you don't know what you're talking about.

Include These Elements in Your Fiction Query Bio

- Mention prior traditionally published books. Always mention the title, year, and publisher. Beyond that, you could quickly mention an award your previous book won or any notable praise it received.
- List any published short stories. If they ended up in a respected journal, be sure to mention that. If your work has been published, it proves you have fiction-writing cred.
- Discuss self-published books that sold well. Such discussion will show that you already have a small (or big!) audience and that you know how to market.
- If you've penned articles for money, mention it. Feel free to skip titles and just list publications. For example: "I've written articles for several magazines and newspapers, including the *Cincinnati Enquirer* and *Louisville Magazine*." Brevity is appreciated here. The agent can ask questions if she wants more specifics.
- Divulge noteworthy awards won. The bigger and more impressive they are, the better. For example, if your manuscript was a finalist for the RWA's Golden Heart Award, that's a big deal. If you won third place in a local writers group contest where the group was so small that there is no chance an agent has heard of it, that award is likely worth skipping in the bio. Use your best judgment here.
- Share if you're active in a national or regional writing organization. Some large nationwide groups that writers commonly mention include the Romance Writers of America (RWA), the Mystery Writers of America (MWA), the Society of Children's Book Writers and Illustrators (SCBWI), the Society of Profes-

sional Journalists (SPJ), and the American Medical Writers Association (AMWA).

- Mention an MFA if you have one. However, simply having a basic degree in English is common enough that a mention will likely not help you.

- State your profession if it relates to the book. I wasn't sure about this one until several agents told me they indeed wanted to know. What this means is that if you're writing a legal thriller and you're a lawyer, say so. The same thing goes for doctors writing about medicine or hospitals, musicians writing about musical protagonists, and so on.

- Your research—but *only* if it involves travel and sounds like something amazing. If you're writing a book with a Native American protagonist, it's not worth mentioning that you have done "heavy research on the subject." That makes it sound like you've scoured the Web and read a few books—nothing that will knock anyone's socks off. But if you spent two years living among the Sioux people on a reservation, that's certainly worth mentioning. If your novel is set in Paris and you worked there for ten years as a translator, then say so.

- Explain your platform if you feel that certain elements are impressive. Nonfiction writers must discuss platform at length (and we'll take an in-depth look at this in chapter twelve). Fiction writers don't need to discuss such elements, but if you're a blogger for a big YA authors blog or you contribute to *The Huffington Post* or other websites or newsletters of note, say so. If you run a local writers conference, say so.

- Feel free to say where you live. It's humanizing, and you never know if the agent spent time in that area before. If so, you have a connection.

Skip These Elements in Your Fiction Query Bio

- Don't say the work is copyrighted. All work is copyrighted. Saying so makes you look amateurish.
- Don't say the work is edited. All work should be edited. Saying your work is edited is another sign of an amateur.
- Don't say how long it took you to write it. Agents are hoping to sign clients who can average a book every one to two years. Saying you took ten years to write your book can be a red flag, so leave this detail out.
- Don't mention past self-published books that did not take off. If the book you are pitching is the sequel to a released e-book, then you will have to disclose such info (but virtually no agent wants to represent a sequel to a self-published book that has not had tremendous success). And if this new book you're pitching has nothing to do with previous self-published works that sold poorly, elaborating on those poor sellers will only hurt your chances of getting the new book published.
- Don't say anything about a desired movie adaptation. And especially don't say that you should play yourself in the film adaptation of your memoir.
- Don't say this is your first novel.
- Don't say your age. This will do you no good.
- Don't say that family or friends or writing peers or your Goldendoodle loved it. Their opinions will not sway an agent.
- Don't say God or aliens told you to write the story. This will get you the wrong kind of attention.
- Don't say you're going to make the agent rich.
- Don't say, "I'm the next Stephenie Meyer" or "I'm the next Tucker Max" or anything like that.
- Don't list your favorite writers. The only time to do this is if the agent put a call out for something specific like "more fiction in

the style of William Faulkner" and your favorite writer is indeed Faulkner.

- Don't say how many drafts of the novel you have gone through.
- Don't talk about your personal life (including family and pets) or what you like to do for fun: "I'm going through a nasty trial separation right now. Besides that, I just LOVE *Arrested Development*, don't you? Buster is my favorite character! Anyhoodles, thanks for considering my manuscript ..."
- Don't say that other agents rejected the book. And don't try to use the rejection letters of other agents as some kind of proof that the new agent should read your work. Trying to manipulate a rejection into some kind of praise simply comes off as awkward.
- Don't say that the book is fiction but partially based on your own life. Virtually all books we write are, to some degree, based on real-life situations, people, settings, and happenings. Saying your book is based on real life does not give it any more weight.
- Don't say that you have children to show you are qualified to be a writer of children's books. On the other hand, if you're a teacher of children, feel free to say so—but be wary of saying something like "All the kids I teach in my second-grade classroom absolutely love my dragon stories!" While that may be encouraging to you, keep in mind that your classroom is way too small of a sample size (and a biased one at that) to indicate how the book will perform in a much larger market.

What If You Have No Credits?

"If I do not have any writing credits to my name, what should I put in the letter?" Nothing. If you're writing fiction, the bio paragraph is just gravy. If an agent gets two dynamite novel pitches on Tuesday morning and one of the letters is from a writer with some short publication credits while the other lacks any credits, there is a 99 percent chance the agent will request pages from *both* scribes. If your pitch shows you've got voice, then agents will want to read more—period.

If you have nothing impressive to say about yourself, then just end your query with the standard finale: "Thank you for considering my submission. I look forward to hearing from you."

FICTION BIO FAQs

WHAT IF I HAVE NOTHING ABOUT MYSELF TO DISCUSS, BUT THE AGENT SPECIFICALLY REQUESTS A "BIO SHEET" OR "BIO PARAGRAPH"?

This would be the one time to simply fill white space and talk about lesser things of importance. It's a tough situation; just write whatever you can, and try to get to at least four sentences. You could talk about your schooling, where you live, what local writing groups you belong to, what writing blogs you read, what your profession is, or anything that you feel may be relevant.

I KNOW YOU SAID I SHOULDN'T MENTION THAT MY BOOK WAS EDITED, BUT WOULD AN AGENT WANT TO KNOW THAT THE EDIT WAS BY A PROFESSIONAL WRITER ACT-ING AS MY MENTOR?

If the agent knows the mentor personally (perhaps they're friends on Twitter), then name-dropping is a good idea. Otherwise you're just listing a person's name that the agent has never heard of.

SHOULD I MENTION NONFICTION WRITING (ARTICLES/ BOOKS) EVEN IF I'M PITCHING A NOVEL?

Yes. These credits do convey the sense that you are a professional writer who has experience with content, deadlines, and editors. It also shows you're in touch with members of the media, which equals platform.

I'VE DONE SOME WRITING IN THE PAST, BUT IT WAS WAY IN THE PAST—LIKE TWENTY YEARS AGO. CAN I MENTION THESE CREDENTIALS?

Simply don't mention the years. Just have a sentence like "I have previously contributed articles to the *San Francisco Chronicle*." Done.

IS THIS "BIO" SECTION OF THE QUERY THE BEST PLACE TO MENTION SERIES POTENTIAL FOR THE BOOK?

There is no perfect place to bring up series potential, so it's fine to write it here, if you like.

FICTION QUERY LETTER, SECTION 4: CONTACT INFORMATION

When you write a formal hardcopy letter, your contact information goes at the top of the letter, centered. However, in a query to an agent, it's recommended that you put your contact information at the bottom—under your name, after the complimentary closing.

This is the place to list a website and blog if you have such sites. This is also where you list your phone number. There is no need to list your e-mail address (the agent already has it, unless the letter was sent by snail mail) or your home address (most correspondence will be by e-mail, and the agent will ask for your postal address if she needs it).

PITCHING NONFICTION: A DIFFERENT APPROACH TO THE QUERY

Those composing straight nonfiction (i.e., not memoir) should approach their query letters differently than those writing a novel. The biggest change you will see is a shift from a pitch-centric letter to a query that, perhaps more than anything, hinges on a compelling *bio*. Remember again that we're discussing all nonfiction titles *except* for memoir, because memoir is unlike its other nonfiction counterparts and is pitched like a novel.

Nonfiction Query Letter, Section 1: The Intro

The intro section of a nonfiction query can follow the same rules as a fiction query—you will explain the book category and your connection to the agent. However, if you choose, you may wish to start off by inserting one to two lines about your platform and credentials to prove up front that you're the perfect person to write this book. Solid marketing credentials catch the eye of agents as well as anything else can—and we'll explore marketing and platform in depth in chapter twelve. Here are some examples of nonfiction query intros.

> I am seeking representation for my nonfiction book, THE MILE-HIGH JUNGLE, an exposé on Denver's growing role in the national drug trade. Currently, I am an investigative reporter for *The Denver Post* and also freelance for publications such as *Wired* and *Vanity Fair*.

> HIDDEN LIVES OF CATHOLIC SAINTS is a religious guide for anyone who wants more information on the lives and miracles of Catholic saints. Currently, 62,000 Twitter followers pick up my inspirational-news tweets every day, and I am the founder of Saintinfo.com, which receives more than two million page views each year.

Nonfiction Query Letter, Section 2: The Pitch

The pitch is where you start to see how a nonfiction query differs from a fiction one. First of all, the seven-step formula for a fiction pitch is nixed. While a query for a novel has to have voice, flair, and style to paint pictures and elicit emotion, a nonfiction query—especially one that has no narrative at all in the story—can actually be quite dry. Your goal is to spell out exactly what the book is about and what makes the content unique and/or timely. For instance, books about great white sharks were written in the past and others will be written in the future. But if you want to sell one *right now*, you must make a case as to why *now* is an optimal time for the book's sale and release. You could make a case by saying, "After last year's five great white shark attacks and the resulting media coverage by CNN, *USA Today*, MSNBC, and dozens more media outlets (full list in the proposal), interest in these oceanic predators is reaching a fever pitch—or should we say, feeding frenzy."

Here is a full nonfiction pitch example.

> While several books have been written about eclipses, no one book has done all of the following:
> - Provided the best high-quality artwork
> - Explained the history of eclipses and the scientists who helped to study them
> - Explained their place in folklore, mythology, and tales
> - Listed all the lunar and solar eclipses to happen in the next ten years
> - Profiled active eclipse chasers
>
> With the release of the supernatural bestseller, FULL MOON RISING by Author XYZ and the upcoming film adaptation in the works, interest in eclipses and eclipse chasing is at an all-time high. I intend to interview dozens of experts on astronomy regarding the subject and to gather the best photography and fine art available to supplement the text.

You would never be able to get away with something such as bullet points in a fiction query, but it works fine here. After the author used the bullet points to list the book's subject matter, he noted how the title is timely and addressed the important question of who is going to collect the images that accompany the text. It's as if the writer here understands exactly what questions agents might ask when reading a nonfiction query—specifically, "What is the book about?", "How is it unique?", and "What is the takeaway value for the reader?"—and he answers them without being asked.

Nonfiction Query Letter, Section 3: The Bio

The bio is likely the most important part of a nonfiction query. The author of a nonfiction title must have (1) the proper credentials to write the book and (2) a solid platform—i.e., a means to sell thousands of copies to people who will buy the book. Since nonfiction authors are the primary marketers of their work, the bio must clearly elaborate on all your marketing channels and platform planks.

In chapter twelve, we'll look in more detail at platform and marketing; here we'll simply discuss how these critical pieces are expressed in the query. Sometimes the bio can require two paragraphs to appropriately spell out, which is why nonfiction queries generally get a pass if they slightly exceed the usual one-page length.

> I hold a PhD in astronomical studies. I am the founder of eclipse chasers.org, and the site receives approximately ten thousand hits each month, while the site newsletter reaches 4,200 individuals (and is growing at a rate of 7 percent a month). I am often quoted in both the mainstream media as well as science blogs concerning eclipses, and I speak at several science conventions each year, including an annual invitation to Boston's ScienceCon.

> I am a broadcast, print, and digital journalist. I am the sole blogger for *Home Post*, NPR's San Diego Argo blog. (NPR launched the Argo blogs in 2010 with the goal of each blogger "reporting and aggregating news about a single topic relevant to the hosting station's city.") As Harvard's Nieman Journalism Lab reported, my blog averages more than 100,000 monthly visitors. I have fifteen years worth of experience on live radio and television, and have close friendships with radio and television news directors, producers, and reporters across the country—in major markets like Los Angeles, San Francisco, Washington DC, Sacramento, Atlanta, and Reno. Specific contact names and media outlets are listed in the full proposal.

These bios immediately get the credentials out of the way and make room for what will take longer to explain—marketing capabilities. Note how each author lays out specific, concrete means he has to market (a blog, public speaking) and wisely throws in some figures here and there (e.g., 4,200 newsletter subscribers). These bios could go on, but for the sake of space, the authors choose to lay out the greatest hits—and presumably explain a lot more specifics in the book proposal itself (which we'll dive into in chapter eleven).

LITERARY AGENT ROUNDUP
NONFICTION QUERIES

"When I receive a new query, I'm hoping to discover that you: (1) have a deep mastery and understanding of your topic, (2) have a long-burning passion for what you are sharing, (3) have clearly and concisely expressed your book concept, and (4) have developed an authentic and original writing style. I also hope to see that whatever you're doing in your career—whether you're a writer by profession or you work in another profession of which this book is an extension and an expression—you're doing it out of a deep-rooted vision and inspiration. Practically speaking, I appreciate queries that are no longer than three to four paragraphs and highlight your professional training and platform."

—Kristina Holmes (The Holmes Agency)

"Ideal nonfiction authors come with an established author platform. Create an interesting blog; it is sure to raise your visibility as an author. Don't limit your publications. Seek opportunities both online and off. Increase your followers, and stay active in social media."

—Dawn Michelle Hardy (Serendipity Literary Agency)

"If you have a ten-point plan to save America, your book proposal should not be the first time the world hears about it. You should be recognized as an authority on the subject you wish to write about."

—Melissa Flashman (Trident Media Group)

"In a query, I'm looking for the types of plans the author has to promote their book. It's a tough business. Promotion is what will help your sales. Books no longer sell themselves. Authors can't just write. If you're not willing to promote your work, most publishers aren't interested."

—Dawn Dowdle (Blue Ridge Literary Agency)

"I want to know what the book is about right away. I would like to see a thoughtful title, even though it may change. I like to believe from what I'm reading that not only is this a great new idea, but that this author is the best author to write this particular book."

—Sheree Bykofsky (Sheree Bykofsky Associates, Inc.)

"When I teach classes ... I always counsel my students not to begin their query letters with 'I am submitting for your consideration a narrative nonfiction novel.' But you would be surprised how many of those I get."

—Andy Ross (Andy Ross Literary Agency)

"Avoid the words I, we, us and our [in your query], unless the book is really about you. Editors are wary of authors who overuse the word I. Unless you or your experience are part of the book, write about the subject, not yourself. Also, avoid the words you and your, [as if] addressing readers directly .... Do that in your sample chapter. The most effective way to sell your book is to stick to your subject and your idea."

—Michael Larsen (Larsen-Pomada Literary Agents)

CHAPTER SEVEN

QUERY LETTER EXAMPLES

Spelling out dos and don'ts can help you, sure, but to write a great letter, you need to see some examples of queries that worked. In this chapter you'll find six real-life query letters that writers used to get their agents. In addition to the letters themselves, the agents who received them explain exactly what the writer did well to catch their attention. No two query letters are structured exactly the same way—and that's fine—but all do a wonderful job of drawing the agent and pitching the story or book concept.

QUERY EXAMPLE 1 (YOUNG ADULT/DYSTOPIAN)

Agent commentary from Adriann Ranta of Wolf Literary Services

> Dear Ms. Ranta:
> NOT A DROP TO DRINK (69,000 words) is a postapocalyptic survival young adult novel.
>
> Lynn was nine the first time she killed to defend the pond (a). Seven years later, violence is her native tongue in a time when an ounce of fresh water is worth more than gold, and firewood equals life during bitter rural winters. Death wanders the countryside in many forms: thirst, cholera, coyotes, and the guns of strangers.

Lynn and Mother survive in a lawless land, where their once comfortable home serves as stronghold and lookout. Their basement is a lonely fortress (b); Father disappeared fighting the Canadians for possession of Lake Erie, the last clean body of water in an overpopulated land. The roof offers a sniper's view of their precious water source—the pond. Ever vigilant, they defend against those who stream from the sprawling cities once they can no longer pay the steep prices for water. Mother's strenuous code of self-sufficiency and survival leaves no room for trust or friendships; those wishing for water from the pond are delivered from their thirst not by a drink, but a bullet (c).

When Mother dies in a horrific accident, Lynn faces a choice: Defend her pond from a band of outlaws alone or band together with a few neighbors and strangers she's been raised to fear, including her crippled neighbor, a pregnant woman, a filthy orphan, and Eli, the teenage boy who awakens feelings she can't figure out.

I have been a YA librarian in the public school system for seven years (d), allowing me to spend forty hours a week with my target audience. The first three chapters are in the body of this e-mail, per your submission guidelines. Thank you for your time and consideration.

Sincerely,
Mandy McGinnis

---

a) I love the punchy first line, the sparc prose, and the gradual introduction to all the book's main players.

b) I also love the specificity in this query—I know who the main character is, where she is, what world she lives in, and what's at stake—without getting so microscopic that the query feels bloated and slow.

c) The letter conveys all the right information but also has a flair for language that promises good writing in the sample to come.

d) I appreciated the mention of her job working with her target audience, which showed some industry savvy.

QUERY EXAMPLE 2 (YOUNG ADULT/FANTASY)

Agent commentary from Melissa Jeglinski of The Knight Agency

Dear Ms. Jeglinski:

I am seeking representation for INK, a 75,000-word young adult urban fantasy set in Japan.

When her mom dies, sixteen-year-old Katie never expects to end up living in Shizuoka with her English-teaching aunt. It's bad enough that she can't read or write much Japanese (a), but when Katie stumbles into the middle of an ugly breakup, it puts her on the radar of Yuu Tomohiro, her new school's arrogant and gorgeous kendo star. After his bullying provokes her to spy on him, she discovers his secret passion for drawing and that his badass attitude is mainly reserved for his kendo matches (b).

But it isn't Tomohiro's kendo talent that has Yakuza gangsters homing in on him—it's his drawings. Because everything Tomohiro sketches in ink comes to life, and something always goes wrong (c).

Now Katie has to decide whether to stay away from the guy she's falling for or face the Yakuza alongside him. And the worst part? The ink itself is hunting Katie, and there may be one person Tomohiro can't protect her from—himself.

I have been previously published as the 2007 Fiction Contest winner in *Room Magazine* (d) and in the Drollerie Press anthology *Playthings of the Gods* (Feb 2011). I have a story forthcoming in the *Tesseracts 15* anthology (Sept 2011).

Thank you for time and consideration.

Sincerely,
Amanda Sun

---

a) When I realized that Amanda's protagonist was an orphaned North American, I thought I might be able to relate to her culture shock issues.

b) The letter didn't overwhelm me with tons of details; it could have gotten bogged down with the story's complexity and left me too confused to request the full. Instead she concentrated on giving me the main aspects of the story: characters, conflict, genre, and setting.

c) This was the line that really got my attention: "... and something always goes wrong." I was intrigued by what that meant and wanted to discover more. The key here is that Amanda had plenty of specifics but still left me with questions that I wanted the answers to.

d) Amanda also had some good writing credits behind her.

QUERY EXAMPLE 3 (MYSTERY/CRIME)

Agent commentary from Barbara Poelle of Irene Goodman Literary Agency

Dear Ms. Poelle,

I'd like to tell you about my mystery novel, UNTOLD DAMAGE, complete at 73,000 words (a).

Mark Mallen was a great cop—before he succumbed to the needle. Driven from the narcotics division and run off the force, Mallen's been surviving day to day in the gritty world of San Francisco's Tenderloin district (b). But just when it looks like his life will end in addiction, Mallen learns that his best friend from his police days, Eric Russ, has been murdered—and Mallen himself is named as the prime suspect. The former cop hidden deep inside the addict is prompted to action, as Mallen sees an opportunity to redeem himself and reemerge (c).

However, staying clean turns out to be the least of his problems. As Mallen struggles to find Eric's killer, a couple of enforcers from his undercover days come after his head, along with a growing number of people that seem to want him dead the deeper he dives into the tangled threads of the investigation.

I am writing to you because I read online that you're passionate about mysteries. I am hoping that mine is one you could also feel passionate about. My short fiction has been published in various online literary journals (d), including *Pindeldyboz, Cherry Bleeds,* and *Word Riot.* I am also a produced screenwriter with another script currently under option (e).

Thank you for your time.

Best wishes,
Robert Lewis

---

a) Genre and word count right away. Good.

b) Atmospheric locale, if done well. I know the Tenderloin will be both the setting *and* a character in its own right.

c) I am a fan of the unlikely hero, and Robert probably knew this as he researched me heavily before querying.

d) His work has been deemed publishable already, so I know he has the basic grasp of craft.

e) Without the specific names of the production companies, I can be wary, but this also generally lends itself to the idea that I can expect to see a well-paced, tight narrative.

QUERY EXAMPLE 4 (NONFICTION: MEMOIR/TRAVEL)

Agent commentary from Alyssa Reuben of Paradigm Literary

Dear Ms. Reuben:

Two adventurers from New York City embark on a worldwide journey through the urban underbelly, taking them from the catacombs of Paris to the top of the Brooklyn Bridge.

Moses Gates, a bookish urban planner, meets Steve Duncan, a frenetic adventurer obsessed with the underground of New York City. Soon the two become immersed in the worldwide subculture of Urban Exploring. This subculture rejects prepackaged "tourist adventures" in favor of exploring the urban environment on their own terms—terms which are often dangerous and always completely illegal (a).

Venturing through three continents, Gates and Duncan find a world of people who create secret art galleries in subway tunnels, break into national monuments for fun, and travel the globe sleeping in centuries-old catacombs and abandoned Soviet relics rather than hotels or bed-and-breakfasts. Together they discover ancient underground Roman ruins, party with mole people, and sneak into Stonehenge—until finding themselves under arrest on top of Notre Dame. It's a journey of discovering what can still be seen and done in today's world of terrorism scares and "no trespassing" signs, as well as a story of an enduring friendship forged in the strangest of places.

The author, Moses Gates (b), is an urban planner and licensed New York City tour guide. His explorations of New York have been featured on the History Channel and in *The New York Times* and *Guardian UK* (c). His website is www.allcitynewyork.com. The other main character, Steve, is a photographer and historian. His adventures have been featured on the Discovery Channel show "Urban Explorers." He is the star of the short documentary *Undercity*, which has over half a million views on Vimeo. His website is www.undercity.org.

HIDDEN CITIES: INSIDE THE SECRET WORLD OF URBAN EXPLORERS is a 50,000-word true adventure and travel story, as well as a subculture exposé. Despite documentaries, reality TV shows, and numerous magazine and newspaper articles about Urban Exploration (d), this would be the first true adventure or subculture exposé published about the subject.

I've written an extensive outline and approximately 20,000 words. The first five pages (1,366 words) follow. If you're interested, I can follow up with other sample chapters and a table of contents.

Thanks for your consideration,
Moses Gates

---

a) This query had a lot of qualities I want in a book: action, adventure, friendship, personal growth, and travel. It was polished and concise, and it conveyed a personal story with an intriguing narrative arc that was set against the fascinating world of urban exploration. To me, it read like fantastic back-cover copy.

b) His use of the third person to pitch a memoir and travelogue might have been off-putting to other agents (most of these types of queries are done from the author's perspective), but I thought it was fine.

c) I thought Moses's professional credentials lent themselves to the book's subject matter and would therefore give the book added depth. Also his perspective would be more credible.

d) I also liked that he illustrated a real public interest in the story, asserting that his book would be the first of its kind to delve into this subculture in the way he was intending. Needless to say, I was immediately interested in reading more.

QUERY EXAMPLE 5 (ROMANCE/HISTORICAL)

Agent commentary from Kristin Nelson of Nelson Literary Agency

Dear Ms. Nelson:

I met you last weekend at a pitch appointment at the Chicago Spring Fling conference. You had spoken with Sherry Thomas earlier about my historical romance, *Proof by Seduction*. You asked me to send you the full, which is now attached.

As one of London's premier fortune-tellers, Jenny Keeble knows all about lies. After all, the fastest way to make money is to tell people what they want to hear (a). It works—until Gareth Carhart, the Marquess of Blakely, vows to prove what he and Jenny both know: that Jenny is a fraud.

Gareth only wants to extricate his naïve young cousin and heir from an unhealthy influence. The last thing the rigidly scientific marquis expects is his visceral reaction to the intelligent, tenacious, and—as revealed by a wardrobe malfunction—very desirable fortune-teller (b). But she enrages him. She tempts him (c). She causes him to lose his head entirely and offer a prediction of his own: He'll have her in bed before the month is out. The battle lines are drawn. Jenny can't lose her livelihood, Gareth won't abandon logic, and neither is prepared to accept love.

I am a finalist in Romance Writers of America's Golden Heart competition for unpublished romance. I currently work as a lawyer. My romance-writing interests may seem rather different from my daily writing, where I focus on law issues. But all good lawyers are, at heart, just storytellers, and I find the two writing practices balance each other. Please feel free to contact me if you have any additional questions, and thank you for taking the time to consider my manuscript.

Sincerely,
Courtney Milan

---

a) At first I thought the whole fortune-teller angle was a little contrived, but she puts a different spin on it with her insight into how well it works in terms of telling people what they want to hear. It struck me right away that this author might be using this plot setup for a different purpose. I was right.

b) I'm completely won over by the time I read the second pitch paragraph. Courtney does a great job of outlining the opening plot catalyst that launches the story (removing the heir from her clutches), of giving character insight (rigidly scientific marquis), and adding an amusing touch with the wardrobe malfunction line. I sensed this work would be witty, and it didn't disappoint.

c) The use of the words *enrages* and *tempts* leads me to think it will be sexy, and I kind of like that in historical fiction.

QUERY EXAMPLE 6 (NONFICTION: HUMOR/PARENTING)

Agent commentary from Tina Wexler of ICM Partners

Dear Mrs. Wexler:

My name is Brian Klems. I am the newsletter editor and social media keeper for Writer's Digest (255,000 newsletter subscribers, 270,000 Twitter followers). Please consider my humor book, *Oh Boy, You're Having a Girl.*

Oh Boy is a nonfiction humor book that walks dads through the early stages of having a daughter. It covers Baby Name Bracketology to The Pink Phenomenon to questions like "Hey Dad, where are your boobs?" (a) It pokes fun at some of the bigger challenges guys face in raising girls but also stands as a reminder that one day you'll probably miss emceeing her fashion shows.

From changing dirty diapers to surviving those epically long dance recitals, *Oh Boy* mixes tongue-in-cheek advice with humor and heart to help psych dads up for the scary, yet incredibly awesome journey of raising a girl. It also sheds light on rules for taking her into public restrooms (Do you layer the seat up with toilet paper or awkwardly hold her hover-style above the toilet so she never comes close to touching it? The correct answer is both) and helps you navigate tough situations, like making sure she doesn't date until she's fifty.

My parenting humor blog, TheLifeOfDad.com, receives more than thirty thousand page views a month (b), while my new Writer's Digest blog is one of the fastest growing in the writing industry. I'm on the writing speaker circuit, giving talks at conferences in Chicago, Cincinnati, Phoenix, Houston, Buffalo, Minneapolis, and other major cities. Also, my work has appeared in dozens of print and online periodicals, including *Family Friendly Cincinnati, OC Family, Southern MOMentum,* and more.

Thank you so much for your consideration!
Brian A. Klems
www.writersdigest.com/online-editor

a) In this query, Brian succeeds where it's hardest: He shows off his sense of humor while maintaining a level of professionalism, and he pitches the content of the book while giving me a taste of how that content will be presented. Too often I receive queries for humor books that are humorless. Or they're funny, but I don't have a clear sense of what the actual book will be. Brian strikes the perfect balance.

b) He also demonstrates his business savvy by showing off his credentials—that's a lot of subscribers, followers, and page views!—and in a way that doesn't feel off-putting. In short, he comes off as a person I'd like to work with: someone who has a strong idea for a book, is fun and funny, and has a growing platform.

CHAPTER EIGHT

QUERY LETTER FAQS

The query process isn't as simple as "Just keep e-mailing until something good happens." We've gone over the basic sections of a query letter, studied the differences between pitching nonfiction and fiction, and seen successful examples with commentary from agents. But, believe it or not, that doesn't cover all the ins, outs, strange situations, unclear scenarios, and plenty of what-have-you that block the road to signing with a rep. With that in mind, I'm tackling some of the most common and trickiest query letter FAQs.

Can you query multiple agents at the same agency?

No, unless an agency says otherwise (though I know of no agency that says this). A rejection from one literary agent means a rejection from the entire agency. If you query one agent and she thinks the work isn't right for her but that it still has promise, she will pass it on to fellow agents in the office who can review it themselves. Agents work together like that.

Can you re-query an agent after she rejects you?

You can, though I'd say you have about a fifty-fifty shot of getting your query or pages read. Some agents are open to reviewing a query or manuscript if it's undergone serious editing. Other agents, meanwhile, believe that a no is a no—period. In other words, you really don't know whether the agent is open to it or not, so you might as well just query away and hope for the best.

If you complete your first novel and have ideas for sequels, do you complete the sequels before contacting agents?

No. An agent will only want to read the first book. There is no point in fully composing sequels before the first book gathers momentum. That said, feel free to draft an outline or synopsis for yourself if you have scenes or a plot in mind.

If you're based in another country—Canada, for example—do you need a Canadian agent rather than a United States-based one?

When I taught at a conference in Edmonton, Canada, I was surprised to learn that many Canadian writers believed American agents weren't open to their work. I talked to two U.S. agents about this (one of whom was my own agent, Sorche Fairbank), and they both said this is simply not true. Plenty of American agents are certainly willing to take a look at the work of Canadian authors. You never know who is open versus who will shy away, so your best bet is to query all possible targets.

However, there are some caveats. First of all, if you're writing nonfiction specific to Canada (or any region, for that matter)—such as a book on the history of Montreal fashion—you are better off using an agent based in that country. Furthermore, the answer to this question really depends on the tone and content of your book. My agent told me that if the story was "a quiet tale set in Canada—all about Canadian themes and sensibilities and happenings"—then it does not cross over and interest American agents. So if your story is based in the U.K., with a U.K. protagonist, and all U.K. characters, even U.K. spellings (*humour* vs. *humor*), then you should query a U.K. agent. But what if the book is set in the U.K. but has an American protagonist or vice versa? Then it spans both worlds and could spark with agents in either location—query both.

If you're an English-language writer based somewhere else in the world—Greece or Moscow or wherever you may be—and have no "plot connection" with the United States, Canada, or the U.K., you should query English-speaking agents *anywhere* that rep your genre and hope for the best.

Do you need to query a conservative agent for a conservative book? A liberal agent for a liberal book?

I asked a few agents this question, and some said they were willing to take on any political slant if the book was well written and the author had a great writer platform. A few agents, on the other hand, said they needed to be on the same page politically with the author for a political or a religious book and that they only take on books they agree with. Bottom line: Some will be open-minded; some won't. Look for reps who have taken on books similar to yours, and feel free to query other agents, too. The worst any agent can say is no, so keep that in mind whenever dealing with a gray area or question.

Should you mention your age in a query? Do agents have a bias against older writers and teenagers?

I'm not sure any good can come from mentioning your age in a query. Usually the people who ask this question are younger than twenty or older than seventy. Concerning an age bias, I would say some literary agents may be hesitant to sign older or very young writers because reps are looking for career clients who have the ability and energy to market themselves, be a professional writer, and compose many books. If you're older, you should have a website—and write multiple books to convince an agent that you have several projects in you—and shouldn't mention your age in the query to be safe. If you admit you're a teenager, for instance, you could be pigeonholed as an amateur without the necessary writing chops.

Can you query an agent for a short-story collection?

I'd say 98 percent of agents do not accept short-story-collection queries. The reason? Collections just don't sell well. If you have a collection of short stories, you can do one of three things: (1) Repurpose some or all of the stories into a novel, which is much easier to sell. (2) Write a new book—a novel—and sell that *first* to establish a reader base. That way, you will create a base that will purchase your next project—the collection—ensuring the publisher makes money on your short stories. (3) Query the few agents who do accept collections, and hope for the best. If you choose this third route, I suggest you get some of the stories published to help the project gain momentum. A platform and media contacts would help your case as well.

How should you start your query? Should you begin with a paragraph from the book?

I would not include a paragraph from the book, nor would I write the letter in the "voice" of one your characters—those are gimmicks. Check out the section on fiction and nonfiction book query intros in chapter six. If you choose, you can jump right into the pitch—there's nothing wrong with that. But I recommend an intro that lays out the details of your book in one easy sentence: "I have a completed 78,000-word thriller titled *Dead Cat Bounce*." The reason I suggest this short intro is because sometimes jumping into a pitch can be jarring and confusing. That said, many queries choose the "pitch first" approach, and there is nothing wrong with that.

Should you mention that the query is a simultaneous submission?

You can, but you don't have to. If you say it's exclusive, agents understand no other eyes are on the material—but if you say nothing, they will assume multiple agents must be considering it. Keep in mind to always check each agent's submission guidelines; a few rare agents want you to tell them if it's a simultaneous submission.

How should you format your book title in the query letter?

Writing your book title in all caps always works, or you can italicize it. Either is acceptable in a query—but make sure you choose one so your book title doesn't have the same formatting as "normal" text and gets lost.

If you're writing a series, does an agent want you to say that in the query?

The old mentality for this was *no*; you should not discuss a series in the query: Just pitch one book, and let any discussion naturally progress to the topic of more books, if the agent so inquires. However, I've overheard more and more literary agents say that they want to know if your book has the potential to be the start of the series.

So, the correct answer, it appears, depends on who you ask. In circumstances like these, I recommend crafting an answer to cover all bases, such as: "This book could either be a stand-alone project or the start of a series." When worded this way, you disclose the series potential without making it sound like you're saying, "I want a five-book deal or NOTHING." You'll come across as an easygoing writing professional who is leaving all options open.

Should you mention that you've self-published books in the past?

You don't have to. If you indie-published a few e-books that went nowhere, you don't have to list them and their disappointing sales numbers. The release of those books will not affect the new novel that you're submitting to agents—as long as that new novel is an autonomous project, not a sequel to a previous self-pub title. That said, if your self-published projects sold well, then sure, mention them. In other words, talk about your independent projects if they will help your case. Otherwise, just leave them out of the conversation and focus on the new project at hand.

What happens when you're writing a book that doesn't easily fall into one specific genre? How do you handle that problem in a query letter?

You have to bite the bullet and call it *something*. Even if you end up calling it a "middle-grade adventure with supernatural elements," you're at least calling it something. Writers really get into a pickle when they start their pitch with something like, "It's a science fiction Western humorous fantastical suspense romance set in steampunk Britain ... with erotic werewolf transvestite protagonists." It's better to settle on the book's core genre and just call it that. Otherwise your query might not even get read. The reason a nebulous genre may pose a problem for an agent is because there's no specific bookshelf at the bookstore for it. It will also have fewer successful comparable titles on Amazon, making it more difficult for readers to discover it. To address this issue, go to a bookstore and look at the titles on the shelves. Then decide where you would want your book to sit if you could only have it in one section of the store. *That* is a good way to determine which genre is most central to your book.

In these situations, many writers default to comparison (saying "It's *X* meets *Z*"—that type of thing). Some agents don't like this strategy, but others find it a concise way to get a sense of the book. That said, comparing your book to other titles in the marketplace or well-known films can be a useful way to characterize the story when you have a hard time boiling it down to a single genre.

How many query rejections would necessitate a major overhaul of the query?

Submit no more than ten queries to start. If one or none respond with requests for more, then you've got a problem. Go back to the drawing board, and overhaul the query before the next wave of six to ten submissions.

Can your query be more than one page long?

The rise of e-queries removed the dreaded page break, so now writers can get away with going over one page. But just because that's so doesn't mean it's a wise move. While going a few sentences over one page is likely harmless, you really don't want a query that trends too long. Lengthy letters are a sign of a poor, rambling pitch that will probably get rejected. So edit and trim your pitch down as much as possible. Get some beta readers or a freelance query editor to give you ideas and notes. Remember that a succinct letter is preferred (it saves the agent time) and more effective (it keeps the focus on the most important aspects of your book).

The exception is *nonfiction* books. Nonfiction queries have to be heavy on author platform, and those notes (with proper names of publications, organizations, and websites, etc.) can get long very fast. So if you have several compelling platform and marketing notes to list, feel free to go several sentences over one page—just as long as the pitch itself is not the item making your letter too long.

Even if an agent doesn't request it, should you include a few sample pages with your query letter?

It's probably harmless. But if you're going to do this, paste the pages below the query letter and do not attach them in a document. (If agents see an unrequested attachment, they may delete the e-mail immediately.) Don't include much, perhaps one to five pages. (My advised length refers to double-spaced pages, even if the pages do not paste into the e-mail in perfect double-spaced formatting.) The problem is that many people ask this question because they have a lot more faith in their opening pages than in their query—the two are different beasts—and it seems like including both would increase their chances with an agent. Including sample pages may help here and there with an occasional agent who checks out your writing, but it will never solve the major problem of your query being substandard. Instead, keep working on the query until you have faith in it, regardless of whether you sneak in unsolicited pages or not. Then you can follow submission guidelines perfectly and not be worried.

If you get an agent to sell your book, does that guarantee you a cash advance from the publisher and widespread bookstore distribution and the like?

Nothing is guaranteed, but likely yes, an agent will lead to a book deal. Some new publishers that have popped up during the past several years only release e-books. These e-book houses usually specialize in genre books (especially romance and erotica) and get agented submissions just like the biggest editors in New York do. Also, some smaller publishers operate on "royalty-only" deals with no up-front advance. But even as the industry continuously adapts to fewer book sales and more publishing options, your agent is your guide and advocate, and is there to steer you toward what she believes is the best deal for you.

How do you follow up with an agent who hasn't responded to your submission?

First of all, check the agency website for updates and the latest formal guidelines. The agent might have gone on leave. She might have switched agencies. And most likely, she may have submission guidelines stating that she only responds to submissions if interested: "If you don't hear from us in eight weeks, it means we are regretfully not interested in your project." So keep in mind there might be a very good reason why you shouldn't follow up—or rather why you shouldn't follow up *right now*.

Make darn sure you are not to blame for getting no reply. Perhaps your previous e-mail had an attachment when the agent warned, "No attachments." Perhaps your previous e-mail did not put "Query" in the subject line, even though the agent requested just that. Or perhaps your previous e-mail misspelled the agent's e-mail address, and the query truly got lost in cyberspace. In other words, double-check everything. If you find no mistake, follow up; if you find a mistake, follow up but be sure you don't make the same mistake again.

That aside, let's say that an agent claims she responds to all submissions "within three months" and it's been three and a half months with no reply. Now it's time to nicely follow up. (If an agent makes it sound like she does indeed respond to all submissions but she doesn't have a time frame for her reply, I say follow up after three months.) Simply paste your original query into a new e-mail, and send it to the agent with a note above the query that says, "Dear [agent name], I sent my query below to you [length of time] ago and haven't heard anything. I'm afraid my original note got lost in a spam filter, so I am pasting it below in the hopes that you are still reviewing queries and open to new clients. Thank you for considering my submission. Sincerely, [name]." That's it. Be polite, and simply resubmit.

If you send that follow-up perfectly and the agent still doesn't reply, forget 'em! Move on.

If you're pitching a novel, should the topics of marketing and writer platform be addressed in the query?

The pitch is what's paramount; any mention of marketing or platform is just gravy. If you have some promotional cred, it and the skills that go with it will definitely be beneficial in the long run as they will help you sell more books when your title is released. But a decent platform will not get a mediocre novel published. So feel free to list worthwhile, impressive notes about platform and marketing skills you possess—just don't let your accomplishments in those areas cloud the fact that the three most crucial elements to a novel selling are the writing, the writing, the writing.

Is it better to send a query via snail mail or e-mail?

If you have a choice, I don't see any logic in sending a snail mail query. They're more of a hassle to physically produce, and they cost money to send. Ninety percent or more of queries are sent via e-mail for two very good reasons: E-mail is (1) quicker, in terms of sending submissions and agents' response time, and (2) it's free. Keep in mind that almost all agents have personal, detailed submission guidelines in which they say exactly what they want to receive in a submission and how they want to receive it. So almost always, you will not have a choice in how to send materials. Just send what they ask for, how they asked for it.

If you're writing a memoir, do you pitch it like a fiction book (complete the whole manuscript first, then query) or like a nonfiction book (write a book proposal with a few sample chapters)?

I'd say 80 percent of agents review memoir like they would a novel. If interested, they ask for the full book and consider it mostly on how well it's written. I have met several agents, however, who want to see a nonfiction book proposal; in addition, some want to see sample chapters or even the whole book. So to answer the question, you can choose to write only the manuscript and go from there. Or you can choose to complete a proposal as well so you have as many weapons as possible as you move forward. In my opinion, a writer who has both a complete memoir manuscript and a nonfiction book proposal seems like a professional who is ahead of the curve and wise to marketing matters—and, naturally, people in publishing are often attracted to such writers.

Is the summer a particularly good or bad time of year to be querying agents?

Generally the "worst" two times of the year to be querying agents are (1) the summer vacation months of July and August and (2) the holiday season at the end of the calendar year. This is simply because a lot of people in the publishing industry (agents, editors) are away from the office. And when they are in the office, they're typically wrapping up tasks and not starting new ones. Still, your query isn't going anywhere. Even if your e-mail ends up in a full-to-the-brim in-box, it will still be considered; the response will just be slower. So don't worry too much about it, but if possible aim to avoid querying during these two times of the year.

When querying an agent, should you include your blog address somewhere even if the blog is getting very few clicks? Or does it work against you if the blog is small?

It's totally optional. An agent won't be able to tell that your blog has low traffic. What she will be able to tell immediately is if the blog is professional, looks decent, and has some quality content. If the agent is interested in you and your work, she'll want to know a bit more about you, so you can talk about yourself and your writing accomplishments somewhere on your website and blog.

At the end of your query letter, below your signature, you'll put any contact info, such as your phone number. Feel free to include your blog URL here, too. Ultimately, if you're on the fence and don't want to direct an agent to your blog or under-construction website, then don't. It won't make much of a difference for fiction writers who are querying. It's more important for nonfiction writers to include social media details, because their platform is so important in the pitching process.

How safe is it to embellish a few details in your memoir or life-story essay—in both the manuscript and the query letter?

You cannot make up anything or fabricate details. Don't add anything if it's a true story. If you went on a road trip and want to "add" a false narrative about how your stop through New York City involved a Bon Jovi concert and falling down drunk in Rockefeller Center, you simply can't do it. If anyone fact-checks (vets) your story and is able to prove one detail convincingly false, then your entire memoir can be discredited.

What you can do in your memoir is eliminate things. If, in the middle of your story, your dog happens to die, you do not have to include that in the book. You can choose to simply bypass that event if it really doesn't affect anything else. So feel free to leave a little or a lot on the cutting-room floor if you still feel like the book is being honest and contains no lies. But a fake character, fake dialogue, a composite character, etc., can get you into trouble with readers, agents, editors, and lawyers real quick.

If you want to write under a pen name, should you sign your query letter with the pen name?

It depends. If you've spent some time building up a pen name identity (website, e-mail, newsletter, social media), then you can send the letter under the pen name. Make sure that your name is consistent on all parts of the query: You do not want to sign your letter "Rita Smith" if your e-mail indicates that you are "Joyce Jones." That will be confusing.

If having a pen name is a newer idea for you and you don't have a substantial identity established under that name, submit the query under your real name. Then, when an agent calls you to discuss representation, you can explain that you believe it wise to use a pen name on your book(s). Make a case to the agent, and hopefully she will agree with you. If not, she surely will explain why using a pen name might not be the best idea.

How do you query a specific literary agent at an agency that has only a general online submission form or query e-mail address?

If submitting via e-mail, write "Query for [Name]" in the subject line of the e-mail to immediately get it forwarded to the right place. An online submission form is trickier. You may not have the opportunity to utilize the equivalent of a subject line. If not, you can address the specific agent in the letter's salutation. You can also have a line or two early in the query stating why you think that specific agent would be a good fit for your work. That way, if another rep at the agency gets the letter, she will see your lines at the beginning and realize that this query truly is meant to be read by the target agent, not simply anybody at the agency.

Can you submit multiple works to an agent at one time?

No. You should submit one complete, polished project at a time. Don't contact an agent and tell her that you have "five completed novels, all of which are explained below." Pitch one project at a time, or else your submission may come off as unfocused and scattershot—like you're pitching five average novels instead of one polished, great novel (even though that may not be a fair assessment).

LITERARY AGENT ROUNDUP
FINAL TIPS ON QUERY LETTERS

"I think the biggest querying no-no I've ever seen was when an author tracked down some sensitive personal information and included it in their cover letter. Eeep! As agents we absolutely love when authors do their research and get to know

our interests, but you want to always make sure that what you include in your query letter is professional and that you don't slip too far into the realm of the personal."

—Shira Hoffman (McIntosh & Otis, Inc.)

"Here are my query pet peeves: (1) When my name is spelled incorrectly; (2) when a query begins with a 'What would you do?' question, like 'What would you do if you came home and found a woolly mammoth eating your daffodils?'; (3) anything that tells me the writer is a hobbyist and not serious about making it as a professional writer; (4) when there are multiple typos and grammatical errors (one or two I can forgive, [but] anything more than that and I start to question how polished the manuscript would be if I requested it); (5) when pertinent information is left out of a query, such as the era for a historical, or whether the book is nonfiction or fiction; (6) when a writer tells me his work is 'the greatest, the best, the most amazing, the next blockbuster'; let me judge that for myself, please."

—Jessica Alvarez (BookEnds)

"I'm not fond of being called 'Sir.' But really, I just want to know what the manuscript is about without having to put a huge amount of effort into figuring it out. It shouldn't be an Easter egg hunt for the plotline."

—Bree Ogden (D4EO Literary)

"Here are the three most common problems I see in query letters: sending queries to agents who don't represent your genre, queries that are way too long and/or include links to other sites where I am supposed to search for information, and queries that include a list of multiple books, many of which are incomplete."

—Louise Fury (Bent Literary)

"It's an automatic rejection for writers who send their query to tons of agents [in the same e-mail] or who simply paste a link to their blog or website and tell me to read their material. I have no interest in working with lazy people."

—Cameron McClure (Donald Maass Literary Agency)

"[Most query letters are] too broad or unfocused. Query letters are always the most irresistible when they're specific and evocative, without hitting you over the head with every detail of the book. Also, a modicum of research ('I'm writing to you because you represented X book, which I loved …') is a nice touch."

—Daniel Lazar (Writers House)

"Do not ask an agent for a referral."

—Karen Grencik (Red Fox Literary)

"There's no need to apologize for yourself—'I'm so sorry to take up your time.' Please don't threaten or beg me to 'make your dream come true' or try to pump up the project in ways that mean nothing—telling me how your mom or friends loved it or that you have 150 Facebook friends, all of whom you're sure would buy a copy. Don't get in your own way! Just tell me about the book, and we'll go from there."

—Holly Root (Waxman Leavell Literary Agency)

On query pet peeves: "(1) Talking too much about yourself and thereby giving the manuscript itself short shrift. (2) Focusing on what isn't relevant. (3) Acknowledging that you were aware of the submission guidelines and then completely ignoring them."

—Laura Bradford (Bradford Literary Agency)

"Queries that put up red flags say things like, 'I made this story up for my grandchildren, and they love it!' or 'I don't know anything about children or writing, but I've always wanted to be a writer.' Conversely, showing you take your writing seriously and know the industry by attending SCBWI or other writing conferences, being in a writers group, or having an MFA in writing from a reputable school make your query stand out."

—Quinlan Lee (formerly of Adams Literary)

"Even though I accept online queries, I still want the query to come in somewhere close to one page. I think that writers often think that because it's online, I have no way of knowing that it's more than a page. Believe me, I do. Queries that are concise and compelling are the most intriguing."

—Regina Brooks (Serendipity Literary Agency)

"The number one query letter mistake is not telling me what the book is about. This includes being so vague that after a paragraph of description, I still can't identify basic plot elements. It includes pasting the first five pages of the novel into the body of an e-mail with absolutely no cover letter. It includes sending me an e-mail informing me that your cover letter and synopsis are in the attached documents. It includes letting me know that you're writing a novel but, in place of a pitch, you would like to send me a short story featuring the same protagonist. It includes telling me all about you and your reasons for writing the novel but nothing about the book itself. These are all query letters that do not function as query letters. A good query letter should mimic the hardcover-flap copy or paperback-cover copy you would expect to see on your book, should it be published. That's because, ideally, your query letter becomes your agent's pitch letter, which becomes your editor's catalog copy, which becomes your book's flap copy."

—Stacia Decker (Donald Maass Literary Agency)

"The number one mistake I see with query letters is simply querying too early—before their writing and their book has matured to the point it needs to [reach]. Finding an agent should be the last step, not the first. If the book is truly wonderful and fully baked, the author will be able to find an effective advocate for it. Most people ... are [querying] well before their work can stand up to honest scrutiny."

—Dorian Karchmar (William Morris Endeavor Entertainment)

"A mistake [writers make] in queries is telling me what happens without spending time allowing me to invest in the character. Without that connection, I don't care what happens. I also hate being told that everything out there (in the market) is bad or that the author couldn't find anything good to read so they decided to write a book themselves. It's insulting to me and to my clients."

—Kate Schafer Testerman (kt literary)

STARTING YOUR

FIRST CHAPTER RIGHT

If an agent gets past your query and synopsis, she'll read and consider your first pages or chapters. This is called "requesting a partial" and usually involves the agent asking for a sample of twenty-five to fifty double-spaced pages. Sometimes the agent asks you to paste your pages in the initial e-mail correspondence, and sometimes she asks for solely a query first, only to ask for first chapters *after* the query gets her attention. No matter how the process goes, the key hurdle you face when an agent is reading your first chapters is making sure she likes what she sees.

So it's vital to start your story strong, but the stakes are even higher than you might imagine. Let me share a dirty little secret that no one likes to talk about: Much more often than not, *agents are looking for any reason to reject you.* This is sad and frustrating but true. It all comes back to the daily responsibilities of an agent: They're so incredibly busy that they don't have much time to review query letters from new writers. As a result, an agent is looking for any mistake, any flaw, any chink in the armor—a reason to say no and cut that pile of letters down by one.

Making the process even more difficult for writers these days is the dark side of the Internet. While the Web has allowed you the ease of submitting queries widely and quickly, that "good news" for you is bad news when you consider that everyone everywhere has that same ease and that agents' slush piles are getting bigger and bigger every year.

You can't control everything as you try to overcome agents' trigger-happy tendency toward "no" and the growing competition of other writers, but you can certainly do your best not to fall into any of the three most common traps that cause an agent to stop reading and reject your work.

1. The book starts slow.
2. The book starts outside-in and not inside-out.
3. The book has an information dump.

Let's look at each trap—and how to avoid it.

CHAPTER ONE CHECKLIST
by Elizabeth Kracht (Kimberley Cameron & Associates)

This is a list of all the things that I notice and think about when I start to read a first chapter.

1. Is there too much description?
2. Do I feel grounded in the setting? (Do I know where I am?)
3. Am I invested in the characters?
4. Is the genre clear?
5. Is there too much backstory?
6. Does it start in the right place, or is there too much lead-in?
7. Am I having trouble tracking characters?
8. Am I being forced to pay attention to characters I'll never see again?

9. Is the pacing too slow? Does the character take five paragraphs to cross a room with nothing really happening in between?
10. Are the characters cliché?
11. Is the chapter too long or short?
12. Is the dialogue sharp, fast-paced, and free of unnecessary tags and attributions?
13. Is the manuscript formatted correctly?
14. Is the voice over the top (commonly an issue in first-person narratives)?
15. Do I have a strong sense of story and character arc?
16. Is there enough happening in the chapter?
17. Is the writing inspired?

Good writing involves covering all of the bases above and more.

DOES YOUR BOOK START TOO SLOW?

Think of a busybody business professional texting with one hand while scrolling through e-mail on a computer with the other hand—all in front of a high-definition television. It's going to be pretty difficult to get him to sit down and read a book, right? Today's successful writers realize that, now more than ever, it's imperative to grab someone's attention quickly and pull him into your story or world. No longer can books "get good on page 44" or "really start to cook in the fourth chapter when all hell breaks loose." A book has to grab us from the first chapter, page, paragraph—and even sentence. There is no time to waste.

I once heard a successful novelist describe what he believed to be the cliché, unoriginal opening to many people's first novels. Paraphrased, it went something like this.

> The main character wakes up from a dream—sometimes to an alarm going off or a phone call. She meanders around her apartment or slowly travels to work, thinking about her lackluster

situation in life and who she's mad at and what happened to her recently. She always finds a way to describe the weather—how it's raining or how the sunlight is illuminating something or how the sky is azure. And then, finally on page 7, there is a scene where two characters interact outside of the house.

What's the message here? Get your characters moving. Even more important, get them outside of their own heads. Construct a *scene*. Create an interaction where something of importance is happening. Feel free to have the character(s) be in the middle of something happening.

Immediately when reading a book, readers—agents or everyday people—need to feel there is some kind of tension, trouble, problem, or conflict. These elements keep people reading. Keep in mind that "conflict on page 1" does not mean a gun to someone's head (though that tends to work). It also doesn't imply you should start with heavy action, like a battle scene. Just aim for some kind of scene where things aren't all peachy—where there's something beyond the ho-hum conflict of the girl in the previous example.

For example, a couple just sat down to dinner at a fancy restaurant for their usual date night dinner. The wife says, "Did you order the veal the last time we were here? I want to order it but can't remember if I liked it or not. Oh heck, I think I'll go for it and just get the veal again." Then the husband wipes sweat from his brow and says, "Uh, honey … we need to talk. I'm joining the seminary."

Boom. You have a problem on the first half of page 1. There is conflict here. It's neither a battle sequence nor a gun to someone's head, but you're immediately showing us tension and also creating questions in our heads: *Why is he joining the seminary? Did she not see this coming at all? How long have they been married? What will she do?*

Don't wait until the middle of your novel to drop us into the heart of the problem. One of the most common things agents say about the work of aspiring writers is that the first five to forty pages of the manuscript should be cut. The trick is to start the book in a place where the story is already moving and give the reader crucial details here and there so that we're not confused even though things are moving fast.

Consider these two potential beginnings to a middle-grade novel.

- **FIRST OPTION:** A narration inside the mind of a boy headed to summer camp reveals that he's depressed that he has to go and he's not speaking to anyone in the car. He's thinking about the jerks—and the love interest—who will be at camp.
- **SECOND OPTION:** "An hour hadn't gone by at Camp Skylight before someone slapped me across the back of the head. The first thing I focused on was the pain. All I wished for in the whole world was that a second slap wouldn't come. One slap was an accident or a bully having some fun. Two slaps meant a fight—no doubt about it. The second slap came about four seconds after the first. It was going to be a long summer."

Which of these two books would interest you more after reading the first paragraph? I'd guess almost everyone would say the second option. After all, why do we need ruminations on the car ride over? Just get us to the scene where the kid finds himself in over his head while facing a bully.

DOES YOUR BOOK GO OUTSIDE-IN AND NOT INSIDE-OUT?

A few summers ago, I sat with two literary agents on a "Literary Idol" panel at a writers conference where people read their first page and we would raise our hands when we would've stopped reading the submission if we were considering a page in the slush pile. I specifically remember two participants for whom the agents had similar feedback. One story started out with a man stewing in his apartment about something. At the end of the first page, there was a great, jarring line about how the man set down his gun on the windowsill—a gun that we did not know he was holding. The two panel agents both told the writer that this mention of the gun should be the book's first line or at least be in the first paragraph. The second submission had the same issue: A fantastic potential first line—something like "I was forced to grow up at such an early age that I have no true memories of my childhood"—was pushed too far down in the text.

These great opening lines were buried—all because of the simple fact that writers do not start their books with the best, most carefully chosen words and hook us immediately. Then it hit me: Holy cow! Maybe examining the start of a movie could help writers understand this problem.

For example, this is how the 1994 film *True Lies* begins (I'll be a bit broad).

> It's dark. We see tall trees at night. So it's not just dark—it's nighttime, outdoors. More specifically: an empty wintery landscape. Snow everywhere. In the distance is the only real thing to see: a big mansion—a grand chateau with warm yellow lights seen from a distance through the windows. The moonlight reflects off the white snow everywhere. Closer to the mansion is an iron gate that seems to run alongside a river or lake. That water is frozen over. Patrolling the snowy grounds near this gate are guards—a closer look reveals that the guards have machine guns and some of them walk with snarling guard dogs. Away from the guards, the ice cracks in a tiny spot as a very big knife cuts through from below. From the tiny hole in the ice pops the head of a secret agent in black scuba gear.

This is how the *movies* get to start a story. This is not how a *novel* should start. A movie can go *outside-in*—it can start by circling the heart of the scene, slowly working its way to what matters. A novel should go *inside-out*—it should begin with the most critical hook to the scene and then work its way out to describe what else is going on.

If this story were a novel and you wanted to get the audience's attention, what would your first line or two be? Something like, "Harry's knife cut through the ice from below. His eye line ascended above the freezing water, and he could make out guard dogs in the distance even before the fog in his scuba mask cleared." Once the audience is hooked, the story can slowly move outward, engineering the beats of the movie in reverse. The whole start to your novel could look like this.

- Harry's knife cuts through the ice. (intrigue)
- Harry secretly emerges from the freezing water. (danger)
- Mention the guard dogs. (more danger)
- Mention the men with automatic weapons. (more danger)
- Mention the chateau. (Harry's desired destination)
- Mention nighttime.
- Mention the snow, the reflection, the darkness, the beauty of a European countryside in the winter, etc. Perhaps here you would even mention that the location is actually Switzerland.

That's how you take an opening and make it go inside-out. If you begin your novel with two paragraphs describing the trees and night and moonlight and then spend another two paragraphs describing the chateau and the yellow light and the winter landscape, then the agent reading it will never even get to the semi-good part—the guys with guns—let alone the true hook line about the man on a secret mission cutting through the frozen river.

"You need to give people a reason to turn the page. Otherwise, they will walk away."

—Kimiko Nakamura (Dee Mura Literary)

DOES YOUR BOOK HAVE AN INFORMATION DUMP AT THE BEGINNING?

An "information dump" is a situation where the author fills in a lot of description and backstory before the story starts to move.

For example, a manuscript begins when the main character, Jody Miller, is being arraigned in court. The judge says that she's now had three DUIs in one year and must serve time in a minimum-security prison. Jody asks for mercy and gets none. The gavel bangs down, and Jody's destination is clear: jail.

That's an interesting beginning. It started in the middle of the story, and all kinds of interesting questions were raised in readers' minds. You resisted the urge to start two days earlier when Jody wakes up from a dream, has a long day at work where we meet minor characters in her circle of friends, and gets into an accident that night.

But—an information dump will derail any great start, including this one. So let's continue with this hypothetical manuscript. Right after Jody is arraigned, the author starts explaining things.

- What Jody looks like
- The shape of her face and nose
- Her hair color
- What she does for a living
- Her height and possibly her dress size
- Her age
- Where she went to school
- What she likes and dislikes
- Her dating situation
- The irony of the fact that her godfather is a judge

This collection of details makes for an information dump, plain and simple—and it's exactly what you want to avoid. But that's just the beginning. The author also describes the detailed looks and backstory of every other character that's introduced for a chapter or two. It's as if the author began his story well, only to abruptly stop and turn directly toward the reader, saying, "Hi there. We're going to stop the story for fifteen minutes so I can fill you in on all the things I believe you need to know."

One of the main problems with a dump like that is that the author is *telling*, and one of the most common pieces of advice to novelists is "Show, don't tell." Don't tell us that Jody is mad at her boyfriend, Matt. Have Matt greet her outside the prison so we can watch them get into a spat with years of unsaid things finally being said in those crucial moments. Instead of explaining, set up a scene and let the characters loose.

Writers have a lot of trouble pruning down their prose and avoiding an information dump. I imagine that movies are to blame for this. If you're watching a film and the main character walks into the room, so much information can be passed along very quickly—from everything about her looks to her age, to what she does for a living, to her general morale. The picture paints a thousand words. So writers feel the need to lay out so much about characters as they are introduced, assuming that if they did not do so, the reader would be confused and stop reading. Also, many writing exercises urge authors to describe characters in depth and flesh out their backstory, and writers may wrongly think this means they have to include that much detail in lump sums in their book.

But that's not true, is it? Personally, when I read a new book, I like to know if the person controlling the narrative on page 1 is male or female, adult or child. Besides that, you have me. The key to locking me in is to keep the story moving and to tell me details slowly, organically—on a *need-to-know basis*. Just ask yourself, "Does the reader really need to know at this moment that her age is thirty-seven? Is this a logical place for Jody to mention her age, or does it feel slightly forced?" Consider these two options.

1. A line at the beginning such as: "But that's just me, Jody Miller, thirty-seven years old and still having lots of fun with my life."
2. An exchange with a prison guard where the guard says, "Honey, if you're thirty-seven and you aren't married yet, you ain't ever getting hitched."

Note how the second way is *showing*, not telling. The mention of her age came about organically—and served double duty by explaining not only that she's thirty-seven and unmarried but also suggesting a potential relationship with the guard.

Years ago, while playwriting, I saw a play where there was only one cast member on the stage—a woman standing front and center. She was addressing the audience directly while holding a bag in her arms that only she could see inside of. I remember that the play started like this.

1. The woman tells you that she was recently diagnosed with terminal cancer and is dying. She vents for a few minutes that she is not prepared for death and is very scared that she has little time to live.
2. She quickly glances inside her bag.
3. The woman tells you she has two children and no idea how to explain to them that she will not be around to witness their next birthdays. She feels like a bad mother but can't explain why.
4. She quickly glances inside her bag.
5. The woman tells you that she now has no faith that God actually exists—for what kind of God would take a loving mother away from sweet young children? She talks more about her big questions about life and the afterlife and what happens when her time in this world is done.
6. She quickly glances inside her bag.

And even though this woman is looking right into your eyes and explaining that she will cease to exist on the planet Earth in a matter of weeks, the only thing you are wondering is—*What's in the bag?*

This play proves that the one thing she did *not* tell you was somehow more interesting than all the things she *did* tell you. Humans tend to want what we cannot have. The unexplained is interesting. In other words, do not underestimate the value of having the reader ask questions. Indeed, it is the questions, uncertainty, confusion, intrigue, and perplexing notions that actually propel the reader forward. That's why we use cliff-hangers at the end of chapters.

When writers list all the details, descriptions, and backstory at the beginning of a novel in an information dump, they aim to help the reader, but in fact they're *hurting* the reader's experience—and their own chances of getting the book in front of readers in the first place.

LITERARY AGENT ROUNDUP

CHAPTER ONE PROBLEMS AND FALSE STARTS

FALSE BEGINNINGS

"I don't like it when the main character dies at the end of chapter one. Why did I just spend all this time with this character? I feel cheated."

—Cricket Freeman (The August Agency)

"I dislike opening scenes that you think are real; then the protagonist wakes up. It makes me feel cheated."

—Laurie McLean (Fuse Literary)

PROLOGUES

"I'm not a fan of prologues, preferring to find myself in the midst of a moving plot on page 1 rather than being kept outside of it or eased into it."

—Michelle Andelman (Regal Literary)

"Most agents hate prologues. Just make the first chapter relevant and well written."

—Andrea Brown (Andrea Brown Literary Agency)

"Prologues are usually a lazy way to give backstory chunks to the reader and can be handled with more finesse throughout the story. Damn the prologue; full speed ahead!"

—Laurie McLean (Fuse Literary)

"I'm not a big fan of prologues; I'd rather be immersed in the book's action right from the beginning."

—Jennifer De Chiara (Jennifer De Chiara Literary)

EXPOSITION AND DESCRIPTION

"Perhaps my biggest pet peeve with an opening chapter is when an author features too much exposition—when they go beyond what is necessary for simply 'setting the scene.' I want to feel as if I'm in the hands of a master storyteller, and starting a story with long, flowery, overly descriptive sentences (kind of like this one) makes the writer seem amateurish and the story contrived. Of course, an equally jarring beginning can be nearly as off-putting, and I hesitate to read on if I'm feeling disoriented by the fifth page. I enjoy when writers can find a good balance between exposition and mystery. Too much accounting always ruins the mystery of a novel, and the unknown is what propels us to read further."

—Peter Miller (Global Lion Intellectual Property Management)

"The [adjective] [adjective] sun rose in the [adjective] [adjective] sky, shedding its [adjective] light across the [adjective] [adjective] [adjective] land."

—Chip MacGregor (MacGregor Literary)

"I dislike endless 'laundry list' character descriptions. For example: 'She had eyes the color of a summer sky and long blonde hair that fell in ringlets past her shoulders. Her petite nose was the perfect size for her heart shaped face. Her azure dress— with the empire waist and long, tight sleeves—sported tiny pearl buttons down the bodice. Ivory lace peeked out of the hem in front.' Blah, blah. Who cares? Work it into the story."

—Laurie McLean (Fuse Literary)

CHARACTERS AND BACKSTORY

"I don't like descriptions of the characters where writers make them too perfect. Heroines (and heroes) who are described physically as being virtually unflawed come across as unrelatable and boring. No 'flowing, windswept golden locks,' no 'eyes as blue as the sky,' no 'willowy, perfect figures.'"

—Laura Bradford (Bradford Literary Agency)

"Many writers express the character's backstory before they get to the plot. Good writers will go back and cut that stuff out and get right to the plot. The character's backstory stays with them—it's in their DNA."

—Adam Chromy (Movable Type Management)

"I'm turned off when a writer feels the need to fill in all the backstory before starting the story; a story that opens on the protagonist's mental reflection of their situation is a red flag."

—Stephany Evans (FinePrint Literary Management)

"One of the biggest problems is the 'information dump' in the first few pages, where the author is trying to tell us everything we supposedly need to know to understand the story. Getting to know characters in a story is like getting to know people in real life. You find out their personality and details of their life over time."

—Rachelle Gardner (Books and Such Literary)

VOICE

"I know this may sound obvious, but too much 'telling' versus 'showing' in the first chapter is a definite warning sign for me. The first chapter should present a compelling scene, not a road map for the rest of the book. The goal is to make the reader curious about your characters, to fill their heads with questions that must be answered, not to fill them in on exactly where, when, who, and how."

—Emily Sylvan Kim (Prospect Agency)

"I hate reading purple prose—describing something so beautifully that has nothing to do with the actual story."

—Cherry Weiner (Cherry Weiner Literary)

"Grammatical errors are an obvious one, but you would be surprised how many do get through."

—Ellsabeth Weed (Weed Literary)

"A cheesy hook drives me nuts. They say 'Open with a hook!' to grab the reader. That's true, but there's a fine line between an intriguing hook and one that's just silly. An example of a silly hook would be opening with a line of overtly sexual dialogue."

—Daniel Lazar (Writers House)

"I don't like an opening line that's 'My name is ...' introducing the narrator to the reader so blatantly. There are far better ways in chapter one to establish an instant connection between narrator and reader."

—Michelle Andelman (Regal Literary)

"Sometimes a reasonably good writer will create an interesting character and describe him in a compelling way, but then he'll turn out to be some unimportant bit player."

—Ellen Pepus (Signature Literary Agency)

STARTING TOO SLOW

"[I dislike] characters that are moving around doing little things, but essentially nothing: washing dishes and thinking, staring out the window and thinking, tying shoes, thinking."

—Daniel Lazar (Writers House)

"I don't really like 'first day of school' beginnings, 'from the beginning of time,' or 'once upon a time.' Specifically, I dislike a chapter one in which nothing happens."

—Jessica Regel (Foundry Literary + Media)

IN ROMANCE

"I can't stand this scenario: A woman is awakened to find a strange man in her bedroom—and then automatically finds him attractive. I'm sorry, but if I awoke to a strange man in my bedroom, I'd be reaching for a weapon—not admiring the view."

—Kristin Nelson (Nelson Literary Agency)

IN SCIENCE FICTION

"[I dislike] a science fiction novel that spends the first two pages describing the strange landscape."

—Chip MacGregor (MacGregor Literary)

"Science fiction is a fantastic genre for showcasing complex, rich world building. But that doesn't mean first pages should come at the expense of character development. Forgetting those characters means readers lose their lifeline for appreciating the world they inhabit, and there will be little to propel the story forward. Also, some science fiction might include a unique lexicon, but it's not engaging or productive to begin first pages with a vocab lesson."

—Kaylee Davis (Dee Mura Literary)

IN CRIME FICTION

"Someone squinting into the sunlight with a hangover in a crime novel: good grief—been done a million times."

—Chip MacGregor (MacGregor Literary)

IN FANTASY

"Cliché openings in fantasy can include an opening scene set in a battle (and my peeve is that I don't know any of the characters yet so why should I care about this battle?) or [in] a pastoral scene where the protagonist is gathering herbs (I didn't realize how common this is)."

—Kristin Nelson (Nelson Literary Agency)

CHAPTER TEN

WRITING THE SYNOPSIS

I've never met a single person who liked writing a synopsis. Seriously—not one. But synopses are a necessary part of the submission process, with many agents either requesting the synopsis up front with your initial submission or when they follow up on your query and ask for more material. The purpose of a synopsis request is for the agent or editor to evaluate what happens throughout your whole story and decide if the characters, plot, and conflict warrant a complete read of your manuscript.

A synopsis is a *summary* of your book, and literary agents and editors may ask to see one if you're writing an adult novel, a memoir, or a kids novel (young adult, middle-grade). Every agent has a different opinion of the synopsis. Some agents openly state in interviews that they're well aware of how difficult a synopsis is to write, and they put little consideration into them. But we must presume that most or all of the agents who do not openly speak out against synopses put some weight into them, and that's why it's important for you to treat this step with care.

And if you haven't guessed yet, these summaries are pretty tough to write. A poor synopsis will confuse the reader, and during the pitching process, confusion equals death. A poor synopsis will also reveal big problems in your story, such as strange plot points, how ridiculous acts of God get the main character out of tight situations, or how your romance actually ends in a divorce (a major category no-no). In this chapter, we'll explore how to make your synopsis successful—which means that it gets the agent to ask for your full manuscript.

SYNOPSIS GUIDELINES

Here are some guidelines that will help you understand the basics of synopsis writing, no matter what your novel or memoir is about.

1. **REVEAL EVERYTHING MAJOR THAT HAPPENS IN YOUR BOOK, INCLUDING THE ENDING.** Heck, revealing the story's ending is a synopsis's defining characteristic. You shouldn't reveal a story's ending in a query or an in-person pitch, but it does leak out in a synopsis. A synopsis is designed to explain *everything major* that happens, not to tease. So avoid language such as "Krista walks around a corner and into a big surprise." Don't say "surprise"—just tell us what happens. This touches on a bigger point: The worst mistake a synopsis can make is to confuse the reader. Make sure that no language in your page is vague and undefined and could lead to multiple interpretations. One of the fundamental purposes of a synopsis is to show your book's narrative arc. Within that arc, the agent must see that the story possesses staple elements, such as rising action, the three-act structure, and a satisfying ending.

2. **MAKE YOUR SYNOPSIS ONE PAGE, SINGLE-SPACED.** There is always some disagreement on length. Synopses used to trend longer (four, six, or even eight pages!), but over the last five years, agents have requested shorter and shorter synopses. Most agents have finally settled on one to two pages total. If you write yours as one single-spaced page, it's the same length as two double-spaced pages, and either are acceptable. There will be the occasional agent who requests something strange, such as a "five-page synopsis on beige paper that smells of cinnamon." But trust

me, if you turn in a solid one-page work, you'll be just fine across the board. In my opinion, it's the gold standard.

3. **TAKE MORE CARE AND TIME IF YOU'RE WRITING GENRE FICTION.** Synopses are especially difficult to compose if you're writing character-driven (i.e., literary) fiction, because there may not be a whole lot of plot in the book. Agents and editors understand this and put little (or no) weight into a synopsis for literary or character-driven stories. However, if you're writing genre fiction—specifically categories like romance, fantasy, thriller, mystery, horror, or science fiction—agents will want to make sure your book has a clear beginning, middle, and end, as well as some unique aspects of plot and character they haven't seen before in a story. So if you're getting ready to submit a genre story, don't blow through your synopsis; it's important.

4. **FEEL FREE TO BE DRY, BUT DON'T STEP OUT OF THE NARRATIVE.** When you write your story (and even the pitch in your query letter), style and voice are critical to the writing. A synopsis, thankfully, not only can be dry but probably *should* be dry. The synopsis has to explain everything that happens in a very small amount of space. So if you find yourself using short sentences like "John shoots Bill and then sits down to contemplate suicide," don't worry. This is normal. Lean, clean language is great. Use active verbs and always strive for clarity. And lastly, do not step out of the narrative—you're telling the story, not talking about the story. Agents do not want to read things such as "And at the climax of the story," "In a rousing scene," or "In a flashback."

5. **TYPE CHARACTER NAMES IN ALL CAPS WHEN CHARACTERS ARE INTRODUCED.** Whenever a new character is introduced, CAPITALIZE the name in the first mention and then use normal text throughout. This helps a literary agent immediately recognize each important name. Avoid naming too many characters,

though—try to set a limit of five or six. I know this may sound tough, but it's doable. It forces you to excise smaller characters and subplots from your summary—and doing so actually strengthens your novel synopsis along the way. Sometimes writers fall in love with a minor character (or joke or setting) and insist on mentioning him in the synopsis even though he is not a piece of the larger plot. These mistakes will water down your summary and keep it from showing agents that you have a sense of what's important in the story.

6. **USE THIRD-PERSON PRESENT TENSE.** The exception to this is memoir. While you can write your memoir synopsis in third person, it's probably a better idea to write it in first person. "Feeling stifled, I enlist in the Army that very day."

SYNOPSIS EXAMPLES

As I did with queries, I want to lay out some successful examples here—this time with synopses—so you can get a feel for what an excellent summary looks like on the page. For this exercise, I'll be using mainstream movies rather than books, but it's all the same process. The third example, *Traffic*, is an excellent example if you're having a difficult time boiling down many characters and plotlines into just one page—I've provided insights along the way in that example.

Synopsis Example 1: *A History of Violence* (Thriller)

[Note: The 2005 film *A History of Violence* was adapted from a graphic novel. This synopsis reflects the movie's exact plot, not the original source material.]

TOM STALL owns a diner in a small Midwestern town. He lives a simple life with his lovely wife, EDIE, and two children. His idyllic world is shattered one evening when two killers pass through town and decide to rob Tom's restaurant and rape one of the customers. During the robbery, Tom skillfully kills both criminals, and his bravery makes him a hero to the local community.

Tom is soon visited by a dangerous gangster named FOG-ARTY, who claims that Tom's real name is Joey Cusack, and that the two of them used to run together in the Philadelphia Irish Mob twenty years ago. Tom denies these accusations, but Fogarty continues to harass Tom and his whole family. Emotionally shaken because of Fogarty's stalking as well as his own newfound fame, Tom's relationships with Edie and his teenage son, JACK, become strained. Edie is unsure of what to think of Fogarty's (somewhat convincing) claims, and Jack, who has been bullied in high school, now decides to use violence against his student tormentors. Tom chastises his son for said violence, but Jack accuses him of hypocrisy and runs out of the house.

Fogarty arrives at Tom's house with Jack as a hostage, demanding that "Joey" return with him and his men to Philadelphia. Tom kills Fogarty and his men with the same precision he used against the robbers. While recovering from minor injuries at the hospital, Tom admits to his wife that he is Joey Cusack and that he left Philadelphia around the age of twenty-one to abandon his criminal past and start a new violence-free life. This furthers the tensions in their marriage, and Tom starts sleeping on the couch.

Not long after Fogarty's death, Tom gets a phone call from RICHIE CUSACK, his real-life older brother. Richie is the head of the Philly Irish Mob and demands that "Joey" travel to Philadelphia immediately or violence will befall the Stall family. Tom drives to Philadelphia, meets Richie at his mansion, and offers to make peace. Richie seems happy to see his long-lost little brother again but claims he has no choice in what comes next. He orders his men to kill Tom. Tom defends himself and kills both Richie and his guards.

Tom returns home to Indiana, but his family greets him with only tense silence. At dinner, the family quietly hints that they accept Tom back by passing him food.

Synopsis Example 2: *The Wrestler* (Literary/Mainstream)

RANDY "THE RAM" ROBINSON is a professional wrestler who gained celebrity in the 1980s. Now twenty years past his prime, he wrestles at independent matches in the New Jersey area for meager paydays. After a show, a promoter proposes an anniversary rematch of his most notable wrestling showdown, which sold out Madison Square Garden twenty years ago. Randy agrees.

Randy goes home and is locked out of his trailer for not paying the rent. His daily routine involves steroid usage, tanning, and loading boxes at a supermarket for extra cash. He also frequents a strip club, where he has befriended a faded stripper named PAM. Following a wrestling match against a brutal "hardcore" opponent, Randy suffers a heart attack and collapses. He receives a coronary artery bypass and is warned that his weakened heart cannot stand the stresses of steroids or wrestling. Randy cancels his upcoming matches and starts to make changes in his life.

He begins working as a deli counter operator to make more money. He tells Pam about his heart attack and tries to woo her while out for a drink. She declines his advances but offers Randy advice on reconnecting with his estranged daughter, STEPHANIE. His first visit to Stephanie's house goes poorly, and she curses him out. Randy later returns with a gift and apologizes for being a bad father. The two reconnect during a walk on an abandoned boardwalk and make plans to meet again.

After Pam rejects his advances once more, Randy attends a wrestling match as a spectator and receives attention from his fans. After the match, Randy gets intoxicated on drugs and alcohol—accidentally sleeping the entire next day and missing his dinner date with Stephanie. He tries to apologize, but Stephanie instructs him to leave her sight and never return. At work, after a fan recognizes him and causes a scene, Randy purposely cuts himself on the deli meat slicer and quits. He recommits to the canceled anniversary match and sets out for the venue, despite his doctor's warnings.

Moments before the match starts, Pam unexpectedly arrives, having quit the strip club to see him. She apologizes for being cold and tells him that he is no longer alone. This time, Randy rebuffs her; he says that the fans are his true family and the only place he belongs is in the ring. Randy enters the arena to applause and gives an emotional speech to the large crowd before the fight begins. As the match progresses, his chest pain worsens. Randy painfully ascends the ropes to deliver his signature move as the crowd cheers. With tears in his eyes, he salutes his fans and jumps off the ropes with the last of his strength, leaving his fate uncertain.

Synopsis Example 3: *Traffic* (Mainstream)

TRAFFIC involves three storylines featuring characters involved in the War on Drugs. The storylines sometimes interconnect.

A synopsis can use an establishing paragraph. I rarely write one, but I did here to explain that this is a complicated story, focusing on one central theme: the War on Drugs.

In Mexico: Police officer JAVIER RODRIGUEZ pulls over a truck transporting narcotics and arrests the drivers. The arrest is cut short by a powerful Mexican GENERAL who hires the resourceful Javier to wipe out the deadly Tijuana drug cartel.

I called the general "General" because I did not want readers to get confused later between the names Javier and Salazar. This simplifies things. Also, you can see here that I immediately decided to cut out mentions of Javier's partner and the hit man Francisco Flores. When dealing with stuff like this, just ask yourself: "Does it really matter?" For example, the General hires Javier to take down the Tijuana cartel—that's what matters the most. The fact that Javier's first duty is to track down a hit man so the hit man can give up information and that the hit man only does this through torture, which upsets Javier—that stuff does not matter. Stick to big-picture happenings.

> In Ohio: ROBERT WAKEFIELD, a conservative state judge, takes a position with the President's Office of National Drug Control, earning the title of Drug Czar. In DC, the outgoing Drug Czar warns Robert that the War on Drugs is a battle with no victory. Unbeknownst to Robert, his teenage daughter, CAROLINE, an honors student, has been experimenting with narcotics and develops a drug addiction.

You see that I am telling the story prefaced by the location: "In Ohio." Because the story takes place in many different locations, doing this makes it clear that we're dealing with another place with another set of characters. I took out the character Seth because, like Javier's partner, you can explain the main plot without him.

> In San Diego: An undercover DEA investigation led by MONTEL GORDON culminates with the arrest of a powerful drug lord. The drug lord's wife, HELENA, only now discovers her husband's real occupation. Her days go from fundraisers and fine wine to talking to her husband through phones in a prison.

There were actually two cops in the DEA investigation, but since they're a team, just mentioning one (Montel) is as good as both. Also, to avoid using another proper name, I simply call Carlos Ayala the "drug lord."

Helena's story, which has an arc, is much more important to focus on than his.

> In Mexico: With Javier's help, numerous members of the Tijuana Drug Cartel are arrested, and the organization is crippled. But Javier soon discovers that Mexico's anti-drug efforts are fraudulent, as the General is destroying one cartel because he has pledged loyalty to a second cartel for profit. This deeply disturbs Javier, who, as a rare honest cop in Mexico, has virtually no one to trust.

> In Ohio: Robert learns Caroline is abusing drugs. Robert tries to fix his family life while dealing with his intense new position in the government. He attempts to have Caroline rehabilitated, but his efforts fail and she runs away. In the city, Caroline steals for money and prostitutes herself to procure drugs.

A lot gets left on the cutting-room floor in a synopsis. In this section of the story, Robert heads to Mexico and meets with General Salazar. It's one of the cool points where the storylines cross and Robert's job gets fleshed out, but there's just not enough time to talk about it here. The objective of a synopsis is not to show the cool writing or nifty story ideas but rather to lay out your structure.

> In San Diego: Helena quickly comes to grips with her new situation and what it demands. She hires a hit man to kill the key witness against her husband, but the attempt fails and Montel's partner is killed instead.

> In Mexico: Javier can no longer stand his work with the corrupt General. He informs the American DEA of the General's treachery and cuts himself a deal. Javier's information leads to the General's arrest. Javier enjoys a children's baseball game in a park at night. His desired payment for his testimony was the electricity necessary to run the field lights, as sports are a way to keep kids out of trouble with gangs.

Javier and the baseball game is actually the final event of the film, but to stick to the flow I've set up, I have to put it here. Ultimately, when an agent reads a novel, she will not be upset if a few events are out of order in the synopsis.

> In Ohio: Robert's search for his missing daughter takes him to the ghetto, and he is nearly killed by a drug dealer. His resolve strengthens, and he rescues his semiconscious daughter in a seedy hotel. Robert flies back to DC to present his important press conference on a "Ten-Point Plan" that will help America win the War on Drugs. During the speech, he hesitates, and then he tells everyone that a War on Drugs is actually a war against our own families, which he does not support. Robert quits his position. He and his wife go to a Narcotics Anonymous gathering with Caroline to support her as well as other recovering addicts.

> In San Diego: Thanks to Helena, a second attempt to kill the key witness succeeds, and the charges against her drug lord husband are dropped. Montel visits Helena's home and starts a fight as a ruse to plant a surveillance bug in her house. Montel is now optimistic about eventually putting the drug lord behind bars for good.

Notice how after the establishing paragraph there were nine paragraphs: three for each storyline, representing the three acts of each story. Each final paragraph shows the climax and the resolution. You'll see that when you cut the number of main characters down to six, writing a complicated synopsis becomes a lot easier.

CHAPTER ELEVEN

NONFICTION INTENSIVE:

BOOK PROPOSALS

If you're writing a work of fiction or memoir, the first all-important step is to simply *finish* the work. The entire book must be written and polished, because agents and editors will consider it for publication based primarily on how good the writing is. On the other hand, when you have a nonfiction project of any kind, you do *not* need to finish the book to sell it. In fact, even if you're feeling ambitious and you knock out the entire text, finishing the book will not help you sell it, because all an editor really needs to see are several sample chapters that adequately portray what the rest of the book will be like. These chapters, coupled with your book proposal, are what you'll use to sell the book.

A *book proposal* is a business plan that explains all the details of a nonfiction book. Since a nonfiction book project is not complete during the pitching stages, the proposal acts as a blueprint and diagram for what the finished product will look like. It also explains exactly how you will promote the book when the publisher releases it to the marketplace—authors are much more critical in promoting nonfiction books than they are in promoting novels. The proposal must prove to an agent that your book idea is a means to generate revenue—that customers will buy your worthwhile and unique product and that you have the means to draw in those customers.

"There are several factors that can help a book proposal's ultimate prospects: great writing, great platform, or great information, and ideally all three," says Ted Weinstein, founder of Ted Weinstein Literary Management. "For narrative works, the writing should be gorgeous, not just functional. For practical works, the information should be insightful, comprehensive, and preferably new. And for any work of nonfiction, of course, the author's platform is enormously important." We'll tackle platform in the next chapter. But first, the ever-crucial proposal.

THE STRUCTURE OF A BOOK PROPOSAL

A book proposal is made up of several key sections that explain the book's content, identify its markets, and give relevant information about the author. All of these important sections seek to answer one of the three main questions that every proposal must answer:

1. What is the book, and why is it timely and unique?
2. What is its place in the market?
3. Why are you the best person to write and market it?

"Concerning how to write a compelling nonfiction book proposal: (1) Spill the beans. Don't try to tantalize and hold back the juice. (2) No BS! We agents learn to see right through BS, or we fail rapidly. (3) Get published small. Local papers, literary journals, websites, anything. Why does everyone want to pole-vault from being an unpublished author to having a big book contract? It makes no sense. The more credits you have, the better. And list them all (although not to the point of absurdity) in your query."

—Gary Heidt (Signature Literary Agency)

Every book proposal has several sections that allow the author to explain more about his book. Though you can sometimes vary the order of the sections, here are the major elements and suggested order.

- **TITLE PAGE**. Keep it simple. Put your title and subtitle in the middle, centered. Put your personal contact information at the bottom right.

- **TABLE OF CONTENTS FOR THE PROPOSAL ITSELF (WITH PAGE NUMBERS)**. A nonfiction book proposal has several sections and can run many pages. This is where you explain everything an agent can find in the proposal, in case she wants to jump around to peruse different sections on different pages.

- **OVERVIEW**. This section gets its name because it's designed to be an overview of the entire proposal to come. It's something of a "greatest hits" of the proposal, where you discuss the concept and content, the evidence of need for this new resource in the market, and your platform. Overviews typically run one to three double-spaced pages and immediately make the case for why this book is worth considering and is timely for readers *now*. Another way to think about this section is to imagine it as an extended query letter—it serves the same purpose. If an agent likes your overview, she will review the rest of the document to delve deeper into both you and your ideas. The overview is arguably the most important part of the proposal. "Your overview is the sizzle in your nonfiction book proposal," says agent Michael Larsen of Larsen-Pomada Literary Agents. "If it doesn't sell you and your book, agents and editors won't check the bones (the outline of your book) or try the steak (your sample chapter)."

"An author must address why there is a demand for her book and why she is the best person to write it. These two questions should be answered very early on in the proposal and stressed throughout."

—Andrea Somberg (Harvey Klinger Inc.)

- **FORMAT.** This quick section (usually running anywhere from a paragraph to one page) explains how the book will be formatted. Remember that your finished, completed product does not physically exist and all nonfiction books look different from one another in terms of appearance. So spell out exactly what it will look like. What is the physical size of the book (if the content dictates a particular size)? What is your estimated word count when everything is said and done? How long after the contract is signed will you be able to submit the finished product? Will there be sidebars, boxed quotes, or interactive elements? Will there be photos, illustrations, or other art? (If so, who will be responsible for collecting this art?)

- **SPIN-OFFS (OPTIONAL).** Some nonfiction projects lend themselves to things like sequels, spin-offs, subsidiary rights possibilities, and more. For example, when I pitched my political humor book for dog lovers, *Red Dog/Blue Dog*, this is the section where I mentioned the possibility of a tear-off calendar if the book succeeded, as well as a possible sequel, *Red Cat/Blue Cat*. Unlike other sections of a proposal, this one is optional, as some ideas will *not* lend themselves to more variations.

- **CHAPTER LIST.** While you will be turning over only a few completed, polished chapters, agents still want to know exactly what will fill the rest of the book. So list all your chapter concepts, with a paragraph or so about the content of each. This section is important because it shows that, although the book is not complete, the author has a very clear vision of the exact content. It also gives the agent a sense of the book's flow and organization.

- **SAMPLE CHAPTERS.** Although you do not have to finish the book before pitching nonfiction, you do have to complete two to four book chapters as an appropriate sample. The goal is to write chapters that you believe give a great representation of what the book is about, whether that takes up a few pages or fifty. Typical sample chapters include the book's first chapter and one to three more from different sections of the book. Your goal is to make these chapters represent what the final product will be like in both appearance and content. So if the book is going to be funny, your sample chapters better be humorous. If the book will be infused with art and illustrations, insert what images you can into the pages. The sample chapters are the one place in a proposal where the author can step out of "business mode" and into "writer mode," focusing on things like voice, humor, style, and more.

- **TARGET AUDIENCES.** You've probably heard before that "a book for everyone is a book for no one," so target your work toward small, focused audience groups. This section is your chance to prove an *evidence of need*. Or, as agent Mollie Glick of Foundry Literary + Media says, "You want an original idea—but not too original." You want your book to bring new, engaging information to a defined group of people.

  For example, when I was listing audiences for my humor book, *How to Survive a Garden Gnome Attack*, they were (1) garden gnome enthusiasts, (2) gardeners, (3) survival guide–parody lovers, and (4) humor book lovers. Note how I resisted the urge to say, "Everyone everywhere loves a laugh, so I basically see the entire human population snatching this bad boy up at bookstores."

  When I was pitching a book on historical theaters around the country, my audiences were (1) theater lovers, (2) historical preservationists in the regions where featured theaters are located, (3) nostalgia lovers, and (4) architecture buffs and enthusiasts. Again, the audiences were concise and focused. I proved I had done my research and homed in on the exact pockets of people who would pay money for what I was proposing.

  Since you identify these audiences, you must *quantify* them. If you want to write a book about the history of the arcade game Donkey Kong, a logical target audience would be "Individuals who currently play Donkey Kong"—but you must quantify the audience, because an agent has no idea if that audience size is one thousand or five hundred thousand. So tell her what it really is, and explain how you came to find that number. You can find these quantifying numbers by seeing where such audiences get their news or information, or where they interact with each other. For example, say Donkeykongnews.com has a newsletter reach of twelve thousand individuals or the official Donkey Kong Twitter account has 134,000 followers—you can use those numbers. If *Classic Games Magazine* has a circulation of fifty-two thousand, that number can help you as well. "Use round, accurate numbers in your proposal," says Larsen. "If a number isn't round, qualify it by writing *nearly*, *almost*, or *more than* (not *over*). … Provide sources for statistics."

"Know your market. This is a business, and the more time and effort you expend in studying and understanding the demands of your [niche], the more likely you'll meet with success."

—Gina Panettieri (Talcott Notch Literary Services)

- **COMPARATIVE TITLES.** This is where you list any and all books that are similar to yours in the marketplace. You want to show that many books similar to your title exist and have healthy sales but no one book accomplishes everything yours will. If you can show that, you've made an argument that your book is unique (and therefore worthwhile) and also that people have shown a history of buying such a book (and therefore the book is even more worthwhile). You're essentially trying to say, "Books exist on Subject A and books exist on Subject B, but no book exists on Subject AB, which is exactly what my book, [*Title*], will do."

    You can find comparative titles by searching through the appropriate bookshelf in Barnes & Noble or any local bookstore, as well as by scouring Amazon. Once you have your list, it's time to lay out the details of each, such as the publisher, title, year, and any signs of solid sales (awards or a good Amazon sales ranking). After you explain a competing book's specifics, you should quickly say why your book is different from it. At the same time, don't trash competing books. Since your book is similar, you don't want your own work to come under fire. Here is an example of what a comparative title breakdown could look like.

The Dirt: Confessions of the World's Most Notorious Rock Band
By Motley Crue
Paperback: 448 pages, HarperCollins Publishers, 2002, 9 × 6, 9780060989156

This tell-all features perspectives from all four members of the iconic and wild eighties metal band. My book will be similar to *The Dirt* in that it details the realities of life, music and debauchery on the road—but whereas their story is primarily told from approximately six different people, our band's tale will be told by fifteen people, thus rounding out a larger story.

"Nonfiction authors need a good grasp of the competition. An author needs to know the category inside and out and be able to explain how his book fits in. I always get a sinking feeling in my stomach when I find similar books that the author didn't know about. Also, avoid saying, 'This book will appeal to everyone!' That's never true, and it doesn't help publishers figure out how to position and sell your book. An author needs to understand who her audience is and how to reach them."

—Laurie Abkemeier (DeFiore and Company)

- **MARKETING/WRITER PLATFORM.** This massively important section details all the many avenues you have in place to market the work to the audiences you've already identified—it's so important that we'll delve more deeply into platform in the next chapter. This section will list your social media channels, contacts in the media, personal marketing abilities, public speaking engagements, and much more. An agent needs to be assured you can currently market your book to thousands of possible buyers, if not more. If you can't show that proven ability, the agent may stop reading the proposal. "Develop a significant following before you go out with your nonfiction book. If you build it, publishers will come," says Jeffery McGraw of The August Agency. "How visible are you to the world? That's what determines your level of platform. Someone with real platform is the go-to person in their area of expertise. If you don't make yourself known to the world as the expert in your field, then how will [members of the media] know to reach out to you? Get out there. Make as many connections as you possibly can."

- **AUTHOR BIO/CREDENTIALS.** Now is your chance to explain what makes you qualified to write the content in this book. Tell the agent things such as your degrees, memberships, endorsements, and more. Anything that qualifies you to write this book but is not technically considered "platform" should go in this section. For example, if you want to compose a book on how to make sure you dog lives a happy, healthy life, this is where you explain your degrees and certifications in veterinary medicine.

"I think that it's important to remember that book publishing is a professional as well as creative business. Most agents are inundated with submissions. In order to stand out from the crowd, therefore, everything about your submission must be outstanding, from the way it reads to the way it looks to what you bring to the table in terms of credentials. It is increasingly important to educate yourself about the publishing industry and to understand the importance of selling and marketing yourself and your ideas."

—Deborah Grosvenor (Grosvenor Literary Agency)

THREE COMMON BOOK PROPOSAL PROBLEMS
by Russell Galen (Scovil Galen Ghosh Literary Agency)

1. **LACK OF A STORY ARC.** Many failed nonfiction proposals are mere surveys of a subject. The books that sell have strong characters who are engaged in some project that eventually is resolved. Don't do a book about slime mold. Do a book about the Slime Mold Guy who solved the mystery of slime mold.

2. **SKIMPINESS.** I like big, fat proposals. Writers worry too much about how much reading editors have to do, and they self-defeatingly try to keep proposals short. Busy editors are not the problem. A great proposal will hook a reader within a few pages and keep that reader spellbound until the last page, no matter how long. Short, skimpy proposals often quit before they can get me, or an editor, truly immersed and engaged. You aren't just informing us about your book; you are recruiting us to join you on what is going to be a long and expensive expedition. If crazy, fire-eyed Christopher Columbus wants me to join him on his trip to the "here be monsters" part of the ocean, I'd like to inspect his ships very, very carefully before I set sail. Editors are scared to buy books because they are so often wrong. Thoroughness builds confidence.

3. **EXTRAPOLATION.** Many proposals say, in effect, "I don't know all that much about this subject, but give me a six-figure contract and I will find out everything there is to know." I understand the problem writers face: How are they supposed to master a subject until after they've done the travels, interviews, and research? Nevertheless, unless you are already an established writer, you can't simply promise to master your subject. Book contracts go to those who have already mastered a subject. If you haven't mastered your subject but you really think you deserve a book contract, try to get a magazine assignment so that you can do at least some of the necessary research, funded by the magazine. But if you're just winging it, I probably can't help you unless you have a superb platform.

CHAPTER TWELVE

NONFICTION INTENSIVE:

PLATFORM AND MARKETING

If you're writing nonfiction, a damn good book won't cut it. You need to demonstrate a comprehensive ability to market yourself through different channels such as social-networking sites and traditional media. In other words, you need to prove that you can sell your book. If you can't do that, a publisher probably won't even consider your idea. I'll repeat that for emphasis: If you don't have a proven ability to promote your work and sell books, then editors won't even consider your idea, no matter how clever or timely it may be.

What it all means is this: If you want to write a nonfiction book, you *must* have a platform before your work will be considered. If you're writing fiction or memoir, a platform isn't mandatory, but it will certainly help your chances (especially with memoir)—and it translates to more book sales and money for you once your title is released. And with the way things are trending, in five or ten years, it may be mandatory to have a writer platform for *any* book—who knows? That's why it's so vital to start thinking about platform *now*, if you haven't already.

To get your platform started—or to take your existing platform to the next level—read this chapter. It's a crash course in author marketing and how to make yourself more visible and discoverable in the marketplace.

"I think it's extremely difficult to sell a nonfiction book by an author with no platform."

—Alyssa Reuben (Paradigm Literary)

WHAT IS PLATFORM?

"Platform," simply put, is your *visibility as an author.*

It's your personal ability to sell books right this instant. It is not "what you would be willing to do," but rather "what you *can* do and what you bring to the table *right now*." I've always thought of platform like this: When you speak, who is listening? In other words, when you have something to say, what legitimate channels do you have to release your message to audiences? To an agent or publisher, these audiences translate into people who will consider buying your book.

If you found yourself staring off into space, just now realizing that you have virtually no platform, fear not. Having no platform is expected. It's the normal starting point. To build one, it will require a concerted effort to reach out to groups and individuals with the goal of building a following. If you haven't done that yet, you're starting from zero—but that's quite all right.

As you get started, realize that platform is simply your personal ability to sell books through:

1. Who you are
2. Personal and professional connections you have
3. Media outlets, including blogs and social networks

The best platform is, of course, fame. That's why it seems like every celebrity is writing a memoir or children's picture book these days. Sure, the books may not be that good, but because of the celebrity's public reach and notoriety, the books are guaranteed to sell well—and that's why a publisher takes the project on. Celebrities have platform—and platform translates into money and success.

> *"The two highest levels of influence are achieved when (1) people follow you because of what you've done for them, and (2) people follow you because of who you are. In other words, the highest levels of influence are reached when generosity and trustworthiness surround your behavior."*
>
> —Dale Carnegie and the authors of
> *How to Win Friends and Influence People in the Digital Age*

But noncelebrities can sell books, too. For the rest of us, the most frequent building blocks of a platform are:

1. A website and/or blog with a growing number of followers
2. An e-newsletter/mailing list with a growing number of followers
3. Article or column writing or correspondent involvement for the media—preferably for larger outlets and outlets related to the topic of your book
4. Guest contributions to successful websites, blogs, and periodicals
5. A track record of strong past book sales
6. Individuals of influence you know—from networking to personal contacts (organizational, media, celebrity, relatives)—who can help you market at no cost to yourself, whether through blurbs, promotion, or other means
7. Public speaking appearances—the bigger, the better
8. An impressive social media presence (Twitter, Facebook, etc.)

9. Membership in professional organizations that support the successes of their own
10. Recurring media appearances and interviews—in print, on the radio, on television, or online

Not all of these methods will be of interest or relevance to you. As you learn more about how to find success in each one, some will jump out at you as practical and feasible, while others will not. My advice is to choose a few and dive in deep—and don't be afraid to concede failure in one area and then shift gears and head full speed ahead down a different avenue. It's better to show impressive success in some areas than minimal success in all.

As you tackle these building blocks of platform, know that such tasks take time. Strive for something substantial—strong channels that will help you sell. Simply being on Twitter and having a website does not mean you have a platform. Those are just the first steps to establishing one.

Do understand that simply starting a blog, Pinterest, podcast, or any other form of marketing does little to help you unless said channel has a sizeable audience, readership, or listenership. Here are some *minimal* numbers that will impress an agent. So aim for—or better yet, beyond—these figures.

- Twitter: 5,000 followers
- Blog: 500 to 1,000 page views a day
- Newsletter: 2,000 subscribers
- Facebook: 1,000 likes

THREE KEY TRUTHS ABOUT BUILDING YOUR PLATFORM

In my writing guide, *Create Your Writer Platform*, I delve into all the ins and outs of the subject and list "The 12 Fundamental Principles of Platform." These are overarching guidelines that will help writers of any kind, who are at any stage of writing. Here I will explore three of the most important ones. The third one is a concept I'm developing as I continue my own journey with platform building.

1. It is in giving that we receive.

In my experience, this concept—*it is in giving that we receive*—is the fundamental rule of platform. Building a platform means that people follow your updates, listen to your words, respect and trust you, and, yes, will consider buying whatever it is you're selling. But they will only do that if they like you—and the way you get readers to like you is by *legitimately helping them.* Answer their questions. Give them stuff for free. Share sources of good, helpful information. Make them laugh and smile. Inform them, and make their lives easier or better. Do what they cannot do on their own: Cull together information, or share entertainment of value. Access people and places they want to learn more about. Help them achieve their goals. Enrich their lives. After they have seen the value you provide, they will want to stay in contact with you so they can get more of this good information. They'll begin to trust your content and become *followers.* And the more followers you have, the bigger your platform becomes.

Always remember: If what you're doing seems difficult, it's probably valuable—and most people will not take the time to tackle difficult, valuable projects. That's what will set you apart and make your content special—that's where you gain an edge, because *takeaway value = platform.*

Let's break down this concept of value with an example. Let's say I spend an entire Saturday at a local park walking and relaxing. I take nice pictures of the park while walking through. Upon returning home, I decide I'm going to share my photos and thoughts about the day with the world, and I create a blog post about it. It has a bunch of good images and some commentary from me about what I did and why I shot these particular images.

Now here's my question: Would you care about this post? Would you click through and read the entire thing? Unless you're a close friend or relative, I'd wager your answer is no. And the reasoning is simple: This post does not provide any incentive for you to take time out of your busy day to read it. If you think about it, the post is actually more for me than you—and that's why it will generate little to no interest.

So how do I make this an effective platform-building tool? How do I create a blog post that provides true value and attracts readers (who can become followers)? I make sure that the post is not for me but for others. So I change the focus of the post. I name it "The 5 Best Local Parks You Didn't Know Existed." I do mini-profiles on each park and add a Google Maps screenshot of each so you can see exactly where it is in the city. I add pictures and explain why I like each of these five locations and talk about each one just long enough to inform you but not long enough to bore you.

Now would you read the post? Most people would say yes—because the post suddenly has value.

"If every time you open your mouth you're talking about yourself or your wonderful book, people are going to start avoiding you like the plague. Think of everything you're doing not in terms of how this is going to benefit you, but how it's going to benefit others. When you're giving people what they want or need, they're going to want to be your friend. They're going to want to help you."

—Gina Holmes, founder of Novelrocket.com
and author of the novels *Crossing Oceans* and *Dry as Rain*

So honestly assess the value you offer. If blogging is part of your platform, consider your own blogging goals. What are you going to blog about? If you say, "Probably my writing journey and maybe just my general thoughts on life," then you may be in trouble. If you want me as a follower, you have to *give me something*. I need an incentive to take time out of my day and follow your postings. My fellow Writer's Digest editor Brian A. Klems runs a blog called *The Life of Dad* (Thelifeofdad.com), which is filled with stories about his adventures raising three young girls. Why do people follow his blog? Simple. He *entertains* us. He makes us *laugh*. He provides value by giving us happiness, and because he *gives* to us, he found that many of his column followers (like me) were inclined to buy his book when it came out. (You saw his query letter in chapter seven.)

Give people an incentive to follow you, and they will. Then when you add an occasional personal side to your outreach, you gain more followers—and loyalty from your existing followers—because you're "giving" again: a small, purposeful glimpse into your personal life and the real you.

2. You don't have to go it alone.

Creating a large and effective platform from scratch is, to say the least, a daunting task. But you don't have to swim out into the ocean alone. You can—and are encouraged to—work with others. Don't be afraid to team up with amateur or experienced professionals who are pursuing the same goals you are or are seeking the same audience or readership.

After I worked on my *Guide to Literary Agents* blog for a few years, it began to reach the eyes of many writer-readers each day, growing to an impressive size. At that point, it became an attractive opportunity for other writers (usually novelists) to compose guest content for the blog in exchange for promoting their books and websites with some links and images in the column. Now, instead of me writing all of my own content (which would take so much time), it's written for me. Excellent! And those writers who create content for me get the spotlights and book promotion they seek.

This piggybacking approach applies to all forms of media. You don't have to start your own radio show or podcast. Why can't you be a recurring guest on existing popular shows? You don't have to start your own newsletter when you can contribute articles to existing newsletters. Always be on the lookout for ways to work with existing individuals, publications, and websites so that everyone benefits.

If you're starting a brand-new blog, why do you have to be the only one to start it? Can you team up with others who share the same focus? Perhaps you're trying to sell a book on gardening, so you're brainstorming a garden blog to increase your platform. Can you get in contact with two other up-and-coming garden writers who want to create and manage the blog with you? The content you all can produce for the blog will triple. Everyone rises together. If you choose this approach, you're gaining visibility at the expense of personal branding. Some writers will be happy with the trade-off; others not so much. So carefully consider your goals, strengths, and time resources as you select your path.

3. If you don't have a book yet, you can and should sell a connection to yourself—and link to your followers permanently.

The purpose of a platform is to sell books and yourself. Once you have a means to market yourself, you can pass along news of your books, workshops, appearances, and more.

But what if you *don't* have a book to sell yet? What are you selling then? The answer is that you're selling a connection to yourself. Sure, you don't have a book for sale now, but you will in the future—so you need to link yourself to interested individuals *now* so you can inform them of the book release down the road. (And as you learned in the first item on this list, you'll be providing them something worthwhile in the meantime.) There are several simple ways you can encourage them to stay connected to you.

- Follow you on Twitter
- Sign up for your free e-mail newsletter
- Like your Facebook fan page
- Subscribe to the RSS feed for your blog

If you get someone to connect with you in any of these ways (preferably in multiple ways), then you establish a lasting connection with that person that does not likely disappear. This means that when your book comes out in three weeks or three years, you will still have an avenue to inform them of its existence and thus possibly make a sale. This is platform, plain and simple. When you speak, these connected individuals are listening.

So if you are wrapping up a speech in front of a group of people, encourage them to connect with you through social media. Keep in mind that people need *motivation* to stay in contact with you—they need to know you'll be giving them something of value. Here's how I will put it at a conference: "And if you're looking for a literary agent, I would highly urge you to check out my blog, sign up for my newsletter, and follow me on Twitter. All those channels include free information about queries, submissions, new agents, interviews, platform, and more. If you liked what you heard today, I've got plenty more that can help you on your journey, just as it has helped many others before you."

LITERARY AGENT ROUNDUP

WHAT *IS* PLATFORM?

"I have a simple formula for platform: Authority + Network = Platform. Authority to speak on a subject (self-help, spirituality, business, economics, etc.) is basically why you are the best person to write this book. And Network is who you know that will buy the book. These two main elements play into each other, and having one helps the other. Platform is literally what you can stand on—what supports you as an author."

—Roseanne Wells (Jennifer De Chiara Literary Agency)

"A platform is the people who know and love you and your writing now, as opposed to all those hypothetical people that will know you once your book is bought and you get motivated to do all of that social media stuff. They're the built-in audience

that you bring to the table along with your book idea—the publisher will be buying both."

—Meredith Barnes (formerly of Lowenstein Associates, Inc.)

"A platform showcases the experiences you've had which qualify you as an expert in your field, which advocate your successes ... [it] is a vehicle for your publicity."

—Bernadette Baker-Baughman (Victoria Sanders & Associates)

"I find that the three questions I get asked about a writer's platform from a potential publisher are: (1) What is their website traffic? (2) How many Twitter followers do they have? (3) How many Facebook fans do they have? Of course, any big publicity hits (e.g., an appearance on a morning show, an article in a prominent magazine) or speaking engagements help—but those three components (Facebook, Twitter, personal blog/website) are key indicators of a person's platform and should be built up as much as possible."

—Alyssa Reuben (Paradigm Literary)

"I define a writer's platform as all the methods the author has of reaching the buyer, whether it's the end consumer book buyer or the bookstore owner or chain buyer. Consider your platform as your tool to discoverability for your book so that potential readers can find you."

—Gina Panettieri (Talcott Notch Literary Services)

PART THREE

GIVING YOURSELF THE BEST CHANCE POSSIBLE

CHAPTER THIRTEEN

ONCE YOU SUBMIT

It's quite a jolt of electricity when you finally hit "send" and the first few agent queries fly through the Internet. At that moment, the world is full of endless possibilities, and your stomach is likely filled with butterflies. Now it's time to understand what will transpire as your query process begins.

EVALUATING YOUR PROGRESS

As discussed in earlier chapters, querying six to ten agents at one time is a safe bet to protect yourself. But when is it time to reevaluate the book and stop querying? If your response rate is 15 percent or less, that's not good—something is not working. Either your query letter or manuscript's first pages are not getting the job done. It may be time to halt the submission process and overhaul your work to give it a better chance. Again, I know that this is a frustrating step in the process and we are all impatient as writers, but it's a necessary task to give your work the shot it deserves.

THE GOOGLE MICROSCOPE

Be aware that agents do indeed Google prospective clients if a query is intriguing. So make sure that "normal," informational things within your control have a chance to come up for your name in a search—such as social media pages, articles, a website, a blog, and more. While it is much more important for an agent to Google a nonfiction author than it is for her to search for a fiction writer, you should be prepared for your background to be checked out. If you have a common name, feel free to use your middle initial to stand out in searches.

LITERARY AGENT ROUNDUP
DO AGENTS GOOGLE CLIENTS?

"If you provide your website or say that you are on Twitter or Tumblr, I will look! I always research possible clients, not only to see what they've been working on, but also to see if there is a lack of information on the Internet, or potentially controversial or harmful information. An editor will Google the author, and I don't want to be caught unawares as to what they might find."

—Roseanne Wells (Jennifer De Chiara Literary Agency)

"I do Google prospective clients. I want to see how present they are on the Web, if any dirt comes up immediately, or if there is anything interesting that the author hasn't mentioned in their correspondence with me. I often find some bit of information that helps inform my decision—usually in a good way."

—Bernadette Baker-Baughman (Victoria Sanders & Associates)

"I always Google prospective clients. I like to see how active they are online and what news outlets have featured them (the more, the better). I also look for their personal website, a blog, how active they are on Twitter, etc. I even use tools like Tweetreach and Klout to see what kind of impact their social networking has. I would expect any editor who receives his or her proposal to do the same."

—Alyssa Reuben (Paradigm Literary)

E-MAIL THE MATERIAL TO YOURSELF

Always e-mail the most recent, polished draft of your manuscript or proposal to yourself. This way, you can access it from anywhere. If you get called away on an urgent business trip across the country, you'll still be able to access the file online and send it to interested agents, should they contact you while you're traveling. Besides having access to it on the road, e-mailing your work to yourself is a commonly used and effective means to "back up" the work and save it somewhere else in case your home computer copy is altered or deleted by accident.

KEEP WRITING—AND PLATFORM BUILDING

Once you start querying, you should, if possible, immediately dive into writing your next novel (or, if you're writing nonfiction, work on building your platform). There are several reasons for this. First of all, the act of sending your work out may give you a pleasant adrenaline rush that will propel you to create your next story. Secondly, delving into a new project is a great way to take your mind off the stress of querying—and stop you from refreshing your in-box every thirty seconds. Third, remember that agents seek to represent authors for their careers—selling many books over the years. That requires you to write many books. So the sooner you have multiple projects to sell, the better.

If you can't muster the energy or inspiration to start a new book, this is a perfect time to change gears and take important steps to strengthen your platform. One of the great things about building a platform is that you can do it during "downtime." Some days, when the writing faucet isn't on, you should blog and make connections—so you can positively influence your writing journey on that day even though you're not writing.

EVALUATING AN OFFER (OR OFFERS!) OF REPRESENTATION

Because agents have connections to the top editors of the world, writers may believe that getting an agent is the key domino to fall on their path to a successful writing career—so they sign with the first agent who says yes. But that's not necessarily the wisest move. The relationship needs to be a good fit to work well. Many writers and agents describe the partnership as a marriage, and you must make sure that you're compatible in terms of goals and careers as well as each other's strengths and weaknesses.

If it's not a good match, you'll have to break up—and that's never an easy move. Parting with an agent stalls your career, and it also puts something of a mark on your record. When you leave that agent and contact others down the road, those other agents may wonder what exactly went wrong that caused you to leave Agent #1, fearing that perhaps you were a less-than-ideal client to work with.

So whether you have one agent offer or several, you can be more certain of a good fit if you find out a lot about an agent's skills, goals, and style by asking them specific questions when you first speak on the phone. But if you've done your homework—researching each rep, looking at their sales, and reading online interviews—you already *know* plenty of info before you ever speak to them personally. So all questions below may not apply to you.

Questions to Ask an Agent Before You Sign

1. **HOW DID YOU BECOME AN AGENT?** Learn about her background. You want an agent who has a history in the publishing business. Almost all agents start their career as an intern, agency associate, or editor. This gives them a necessary knowledge base for their job as well as valuable industry contacts. Good agents do not become agents overnight.

2. **WHAT BOOKS HAVE YOU SOLD RECENTLY?** By learning what an agent has sold, you learn what kind of titles she has the ability to sell in the future, the breadth of her selling skill, and the depth of her contact list.

3. **TELL ME ABOUT YOUR AGENCY. HOW MANY AGENTS ARE THERE, AND HOW DO YOU WORK TOGETHER?** This will help illuminate

whether your agent is part of a larger, powerful team that shares resources and contacts. This is one reason signing with a newer agent is not a bad thing at all—because she utilizes her co-workers for help and leads.

4. **WHAT DID YOU LIKE ABOUT MY BOOK? WHAT ATTRACTED YOU TO THIS PROJECT?** You're looking for passion and enthusiasm from an agent. Indeed it is the passion and enthusiasm that will keep your agent up late working for you to see your book come to life.

5. **WHICH EDITORS DO YOU SEE US SUBMITTING THIS BOOK TO, AND HAVE YOU SOLD TO THEM BEFORE?** If you fear the agent lacks proper contacts to move your work, ask this straight out. The question tests not only her plan for where to send the manuscript but also her connections and clout. Do not expect her to reply with a comprehensive list. After all, this discussion is just the beginning of the beginning. You're just looking for her to have some targets in mind.

6. **IF THOSE TARGET EDITORS TURN IT DOWN, WILL YOU CONTINUE SUBMITTING OR WOULD IT BE BEST FOR ME TO WORK ON A NEW PROJECT?** Some agents only aim to sell books in "larger" deals to sizeable publishing houses and well-known editors. This might not be what you have in mind, so learn her strategy now. It's an unfortunate situation when an agent fields a dozen rejections for a book and declares it "dead" even though you protest that more markets exist. Sometimes all you want is for the book to find a loving home and get released into the world, but your agent wants "a fantastic deal or nothing." Resentment can build quickly if you're not on the same page.

7. **WHAT CHANGES DO YOU THINK THE MANUSCRIPT NEEDS BEFORE WE SUBMIT?** If the agent has grand thoughts on revising the work pre-submission, you need to know that before you sign with her. You don't want to sign a contract and have her surprise you by suggesting you "cut 50 percent of the book."

8. **ARE YOU AN EDITORIAL AGENT?** Having an agent that offers editorial suggestions and gets her hands dirty in the editing process can be very important to some authors.

9. **MAY I CONTACT SOME OF YOUR CURRENT CLIENTS?** Most agents will be happy to pass along a few names and e-mails. But if your agent happens to represent a famous *New York Times* best-selling author, don't be surprised if you don't get *that* phone number. Some agents, though, are more reluctant to pass along names and info. They like to make each of their clients feel extremely special and important. If multiple writers considering the agent start calling that client, it reminds the client that he is simply one of many authors in the agent's stable. (Later in the chapter, I'll discuss what you should talk to an agent's current clients about.)

10. **ARE YOU, OR ARE OTHER AGENTS AT YOUR AGENCY, MEMBERS OF THE AAR?** Again, as discussed in chapter four, if an agent says no, that is by no means a deal breaker. But hearing her say yes is always nice.

11. **WHAT CAN I DO TO HELP YOU SELL THIS BOOK AND SECURE THE BEST DEAL POSSIBLE?** This is a great open-ended question for two different reasons. First, it immediately shows you're a helpful, proactive writer who wants to be involved. If the agent had any doubts about you, those doubts may dissipate for the time being. Secondly, this question gives the agent an opportunity to honestly convey suggestions and thoughts concerning how you can truly make a difference moving forward. Perhaps she'll say, "Start a website so editors know you're a professional." Or perhaps she'll say, "I can probably sell the book as is, but if you can find a way to trim five thousand words, I'll have an even better chance." Listen to what your agent suggests, and take her concerns seriously.

12. **TAKE ME THROUGH THE PROCESS OF WHEN YOU SUBMIT TO EDITORS. HOW INVOLVED AND UPDATED WILL I BE?** This question allows your agent to be up front concerning how many phone

calls and spreadsheets you will get during the process. When you know what to expect, you will not feel like you're being left out of conversations—or bogged down with information.

13. **IF, FOR WHATEVER UNFORESEEN REASON, YOU WERE TO STEP DOWN AS AN AGENT IN THE FUTURE, WOULD I BE PASSED TO A CO-AGENT?** The first thing an agent will say when asked this question is probably "I have no intention of leaving, so this is not a concern." But don't give up; press her for an answer. You deserve to know if, in the event of any circumstances leading to the agent temporarily or permanently leaving her work (such as, God forbid, a major illness), you will have the safety net of being passed to a co-agent. If the agent works alone and has no co-agents, you can ask if she will refer you to agent friends in the industry.

14. **IF YOU SWITCH AGENCIES, WOULD I TRANSFER WITH YOU?** If your agent is part of a larger agency, do not skip this question—because this area gets real tricky real fast. Agents switch agencies all the time. But the agent may have signed an employment contract that says if she leaves, her clients stay with XYZ Literary. If you make a deep connection with an individual agent, it's not an ideal situation to know you legally cannot stay with that agent should she find employment elsewhere.

15. **WILL YOU REPRESENT EVERY BOOK I WRITE?** Just because an agent signs you does not mean that she will be willing to send out *everything* you write. She has signed you based on the strength of the book you submitted, and the ideal scenario is that everything you continue to write will also connect with her in some way—but that isn't always the case. An agent should be forthcoming with you if she doesn't feel that your most recent material is marketable or appropriate for her editors, as it is her reputation at stake. From an agent's point of view, it is very, very difficult to gain an editor's trust—and an agent doesn't want to lose such an important relationship simply because a client pushes

her to submit something she doesn't want to submit. So ask an agent about how future books will be handled. Some agents, if they don't connect with a book, will offer editorial notes on how to make it better. Other agents will simply "pass" on the work and invite you to send your next book when it's complete. Obviously these two approaches are extremely different, so make sure you know what you're getting into beforehand. And if you believe in a book that the agent does not, you have to know if the agent is kosher with you sending it to publishers on your own.

16. **HOW MUCH DO YOU THINK I'LL BE PAID FOR THE BOOK?** Most writers will not ask this question during the initial conversation, and I consider that a *good* thing. I only include the question because some authors—most often nonfiction author-personalities and up-and-coming media figures—may want to know this up front to see if the book will be worth their time. That aside, it's next to impossible for agents to speculate how much money a first book will garner in an advance from the publisher, especially a novel. (Money estimates are easier to pinpoint when dealing with a sequel or second book, because the track record and payment for the first book can help paint a clearer picture.)

Here's the danger and complication involved in asking this question: When my agent and I began to pitch our first nonfiction book together, I asked this question at some point, and the answer I received was a healthy amount. But then several key publishers passed on the work, and our target estimate suddenly dropped 40 percent. More publishers said no, and the estimate continued to drop like a rock. We finally got one offer on the book, which we would eventually turn down. The amount? One thousand dollars. Needless to say, our target estimate was that figure many, many times over. I learned a valuable lesson from that experience even though the book never got published: Have loose or no financial expectations going in, because you never know what the offer will be.

DO YOU NEED TO MEET WITH AN AGENT BEFORE YOU SIGN?

When you sign with an agent, you're putting your literary life in a stranger's hands—at least temporarily. It's nerve-racking. An impulse in this situation is to meet with the agent face to face so you can use your instincts to gauge her personality as well as her enthusiasm for your book. But alas, meeting face to face is not always the easiest thing to do. It costs money and effort to fly to New York or San Francisco on a whim, and it's not like you can delay an agent by saying, "Thanks for the offer of representation. I see on my calendar that I'll be in New York six months from now, so let's get together then and see if we click so I can make a final decision."

Because of these restraints, there is a very real possibility you will not get to meet your agent face to face before you sign, and that's quite alright. I'd say the majority of writers don't meet their agents personally before signing, and some may never see their agent in the flesh over the span of years. But while you may not sign a contract in person, do not pass up a long phone call to get to know the agent. People can hide behind e-mail conversation but not so much over the phone.

Asking an agent questions is a delicate process. Definitely do not skip any hard questions if you have pressing concerns. The agent is used to such inquiries and will respect you for politely asking them. At the same time, agents do not like to be pushed too hard too fast—as if a writer is forcing them to "prove their worth." In other words, ask questions, sure, but do not "grill" the agent or come off too pointed. Again, you should have already done plenty of homework and known this agent was a good fit for you.

What to Expect When an Agent Makes an Offer

If an agent offers representation, that is your moment of opportunity—so use it. Let's run through a possible time line of events and what you should do at each step along the way.

Let's say Agent *X* writes you an e-mail saying she loves your book and would be thrilled to discuss representation. You reply that you're free tomorrow in the afternoon to chat about it, and a formal phone call is scheduled. This is your brief moment of leverage and must not be wasted.

What you need to do immediately is e-mail any agents that are currently still considering the work—those that either requested the full from you or asked to see more materials. It is these other agents that legitimately showed interest, and it's time to light a fire under them and see what happens. Nicely inform these other agents that you have an offer of representation from a literary agent and that if they would like to make you an offer as well, to please reach out within the next five days. "We agents trust and respect our colleagues," says Jessica Sinsheimer of the Sarah Jane Freymann Literary Agency. "If another agent likes your work, we'll believe it's for a reason."

You have the scheduled call with Agent *X*, and all goes well. No matter how good the discussion goes, you should tell her you're taking several days to think about your next step. Thank her for her time, and say you'll be in touch with an answer within a week. This time is not only to clear your head and judge the offer but also to allow other agents the chance to make an offer if they wish.

Sinsheimer explains what to do in this crucial time period: "It is vital you remember that *you* are the one in the position of power here. You have the book. They want it. No matter how much you may feel otherwise, you get to decide who gets it. Be polite and listen to what they have to say, but then hang up the phone. Then go about your routine, and *think*."

While you're thinking about the offer from Agent *X* and all her answers to your tough questions, there is a good chance Agents *Y* and *Z* will write back to also make you an offer. If they do, schedule phone calls with them as soon as possible. You're on a time table and need not only to talk to these other reps quickly but also to talk to current clients from each agent.

Talking to the Agent's Existing Clients

Ask every agent you speak to if they can pass along contact information for two or three of their clients—most will. Aim for clients who write similar books to your own. Talking to these clients will help you understand how the agent operates, from whom she sells to in the business to how fast she sells books to how much she's in contact with you throughout the process. These answers will help you make your final decision. In fact, there is a decent chance that one of these writers will have been in your shoes before, with offers from multiple agents, perhaps even the same agents you're considering. Those writers, in particular, will be a fantastic resource in helping you make your final decision.

Before you call a client, remember two things.

1. If you have most of your questions answered but something is nagging you, make sure to address this important point. For example, if you want to say yes to the agent but are worried her style is too abrasive for you, it is this point that you must raise in the conversation with her writers. Otherwise there is little point in talking with the writers.
2. These writers are busy people, so don't talk to them any longer than is necessary (unless they seem happy to gab). Cut to the chase, ask the most important questions, and thank them for their time.

When you get a client on the phone, after you exchange pleasantries, I strongly urge you to tell the client that your conversation is strictly off the record and that nothing will be repeated—and then follow through on that promise. That way, if there is a thing or two about the agent that the client wants to warn you about, he will ideally be more open to doing so.

Here are some quick questions to consider asking represented writers.

• How did you come to sign with [Agent]?

- Did you have multiple offers of representation? And if so, what made you choose [Agent] over other offers?
- Can you tell me what you like about working with [Agent]? What makes her special?
- How many books have you given to [Agent] to sell? How many of those did she sell?
- When I spoke with [Agent], she told me her agenting style was [X]. Have you found that to be the case?
- Is [Agent] open to suggestions and input from you?

At this point, you have more than enough information to make a decision and respond to the agent. Trust the information you've gathered and your gut feeling. Make your decision, and inform all involved parties of your choice, so you can get the ball rolling and try to sell your book to an editor.

CHAPTER FOURTEEN

WORKING WITH AN AGENT

After all the revisions and manuscript overhauls and query edits, the hard work has finally paid off. You just got "the call" last week and are now a represented author. Congrats—you have an agent! It's time to tell your family and friends, and to update your Twitter bio.

Now that you've signed with an agent, one journey has ended and another has begun. It's time to start what will hopefully be a long-term, prosperous relationship with your agent. This chapter is a rundown of what you can expect in such a relationship and includes advice for establishing a healthy career that you both can enjoy and benefit from.

SIGNING A CONTRACT

Once an agent offers representation, the first step is to sign an author-agent contract. This is a simple document that essentially says she now represents your book-length works and will be in charge of selling them. It will also say that she takes 15 to 20 percent of your earnings (this is standard and nonnegotiable), depending on the deal. These contracts are remarkably straightforward; however, depending on what you have in mind, the following are things to look for before you scribble your John Hancock.

1. **DECIDE ON A ONE-BOOK CONTRACT OR A MULTIBOOK CONTRACT.** Agents can tailor a contract to say either. Most times, agents want a writer for the length of his career, but you (or the agent) can limit the length of the partnership if you both agree. If it's a limited contract, once you sell that book or move on from it, you can always choose to execute a similar contract with your agent for the next book, and your career won't miss a beat.

2. **MAKE SURE THERE IS A CLAUSE THAT ALLOWS YOU TO GET OUT OF THE RELATIONSHIP AT ANY TIME, EVEN IF THERE IS A WAITING PERIOD.** Unfortunately, like some marriages, the day may come when you or the agent or both of you decide it's time to part ways. Thankfully, if you want out of the partnership, agents will oblige, but it's the "waiting period" that varies from agent to agent—contracts typically ask for something along the lines of "sixty days until the contract is dissolved." This is because agents will have submissions out to different editors, and they will want a chance to close a deal (and finally make some money) before you leave. That's why they specify this waiting period. The length of time varies from agent to agent. In my opinion, anything from zero to ninety days is fair. Anything more than that is not. So address this point up front before you sign.

3. **NOTE THAT WHILE YOU WILL BE ABLE TO GET OUT OF THE PARTNERSHIP IF NEEDED, THE AGENT WILL FOREVER BE LOCKED IN WITH ANY SALES THEY HAVE MADE.** In other words, I can choose to leave my agent at any time, but she will always be my agent (and receive 15 percent) from the six books we've already sold together.

4. **AGREE ON WHAT TYPE(S) OF BOOKS THE AGENT WILL REPRESENT.** It's not uncommon for an author writing one kind of book to want to try her hand at something different. You may have a few mysteries published, only to decide you just have to start writing picture books as well—or screenplays, or stage plays, or books

about geometry. But you could be in an awkward bind if your agent doesn't represent any of these genres, yet you're locked in with her contractually to sell "any book-length works." So if you know or suspect you'll want to diverge from your current genre down the line, bring that up early and have the contract reflect how that will be handled.

5. **MAKE SURE ALL YOUR CONCERNS ARE ADDRESSED.** Perhaps during your phone interview with the agent, you relayed that you feel most comfortable with weekly updates on submissions and want the final say over manuscript changes before your book is sent to publishers. Make sure the contract reflects these concerns.

In some cases, you might not sign the contract immediately. While some agents may want to lock up representation right away, others may take it slower. A more experienced agent with a full client list may look at you as a promising author with a book that's not quite there. The agent will suggest changes and guide you through revision, but she will not sign a contract or submit your work until the novel is ready, in her opinion. This situation has pros and cons. Ideally the novel will become ready, the agent will sell it, and all will be fantastic. But if something goes wrong—if the agent finds the novel overhaul disagreeable or if the agent's attention gets pulled to another genre or project—she may leave you and your project abruptly, without a home. Recognize this reality so you know the risk before moving forward.

NOT SO FAST WITH THAT LAWYER

Sometimes people will recommend seeking out a literary lawyer to help you with interpreting rights and contracts. While lawyers are certainly of value in some circumstances, there isn't much of a place for them in the agent-author process. In fact, bringing an attorney into the fray at this stage can gum up the works. A lawyer may not understand the basic agent-author relationship and may have you ask for demands in the contract that make the agent's job harder or make her uneasy. An example is if the lawyer explains to you that her 15 percent commission is just a starting figure and can be negotiated down. (It won't be.)

The agent-author contract is fairly standard and short. Later on, there is no need to get a lawyer to review your book contract from a publisher, because that's what an agent is for. An agent is skilled at publishing contract lingo and negotiation—recognizing things like boilerplates and the need to keep certain rights in exchange for possibly giving up others.

If you have a skilled agent, it's best to leave the lawyer out of deals. Lawyers are best used when you have a contract from a publisher but no agent representation.

HOW TO BE AN IDEAL AUTHOR-CLIENT

Every agent dreams of a perfect author—someone who writes a lot, responds to rewrite requests, and is always pleasant to work with. So if you can, be that writer! Here are some quick tips.

- **DON'T BURDEN HER WITH CALLS.** Sure, you two may be friends and share some *Seinfeld* pop-culture jokes on the phone from time to time, but the fact remains that your relationship is still a *business* relationship at heart. That means no unnecessary communication. An agent's typical day is extremely busy, and she really doesn't have time to hear about how your neighbor is mowing his lawn at 7 A.M. every Saturday morning and waking up your family. Feel free to contact her if you need her advice on a book project or if you're going to be late on a deadline. But don't call her simply to ask, "Has my book sold yet? What about now? What about now?"
- **UNDERSTAND THAT COMMUNICATION COMES IN WAVES, AND DON'T DEMAND UPDATES ABOUT NOTHING.** On the subject of communication, know that an agent's attention tends to focus on

each client during periods of action. What that means is when she's ready to submit your work to editors, that's when your communication with the agent will peak. You'll get weekly calls and e-mails and updates. You'll discuss feedback, responses, and plans. During this intense time, you are one of the foremost things on your agent's mind. But then once the agent has sold your book or moved on to other clients, the communication abruptly stops and may not pick up again for months. This is okay. There will be pockets of time when your agent is in constant communication and times when her focus is elsewhere. This is normal.

- **KEEP WRITING!** All agents say the best writers are the ones that can produce a lot of content (i.e., books). The more you write, the more your agent has to sell, and the more she'll cherish you as a client. So keep writing! Don't wait for an agent to prod you.
- **HIT YOUR DEADLINES, AND DO WHAT YOU SAY YOU'RE GOING TO.** An ideal client always makes his deadlines and comes through on his responsibilities. The only time missing a deadline is acceptable is when dealing with some kind of health or family emergency.
- **COMMUNICATE OPENLY, YET RESPECTFULLY.** While it's true that no agent or editor wants to deal with a micromanaging writer who has a strong opinion about every little detail of the publishing process, it is certainly acceptable to politely bring up concerns if you feel like you can make a valid point about why something will not work. Your opinion does matter—so speak up (nicely) if you have something to say. Let's say your book is finally released—hooray! But then its sales underperform. When you talk with your agent after the launch, you say, "It's no surprise that sales aren't better because I've always known the cover and back-jacket copy were awful and conveyed the wrong themes." Your agent asks why these issues were not brought up earlier, and you say that you didn't want to step on any toes by getting involved.

- **ENJOY THE SUCCESSES.** If an agent is able to sell your book to a great publisher and create a beautiful book, that moment should be enjoyed. Some books will sell; others won't. Don't be an author who ignores all the best moments and constantly finds something to nag about. Selling a book is difficult—so while you can be determined and ambitious, also remember to be realistic and enjoy the successes.

- **BUILD YOUR PLATFORM.** If you're in the writing game for the long haul—and hopefully you are—you must understand that anything you can do to market yourself and your books is valuable to all parties involved. If you're writing nonfiction, then your platform has been a major aspect of the deal from beginning to end, and you should always be spreading the word about you and your work however you can. If you're a novelist, you won't be expected to do any drastic marketing, but almost certainly you will be asked to do some basic tasks—such as building a simple author website, writing some promotional guest blogs, and gathering a list of e-mail contacts for your publicist to reach out to.

LITERARY AGENT ROUNDUP

AGENTS' IDEAS ON IDEAL CLIENTS

"A mutual respect for one another's time and efforts always goes a long way. I always hate asking an author to drop everything and get me something ASAP and feel similarly when the roles are reversed."

—Elisabeth Weed (Weed Literary)

"A lasting relationship with an agent is not a guarantee. I have let go of clients, and they have let go of me. For me, usually communication style is the issue or authors who push the boundaries of the relationship—i.e., try and tell me how to do

my job or when to do my job. I get a great deal of personal satisfaction from my relationships with my clients (more than they know). Life is too short to work with people you don't like or can't communicate with well. I value those authors of mine who are patient and understand that they are never far from my mind, even if they don't hear from me. And I adore those clients who make me laugh on a regular basis—you know who you are!"

—Elizabeth Kracht (Kimberley Cameron & Associates)

"My dream client is someone who believes strongly enough in the work not to be deterred but who can also be flexible enough to take good editorial advice."

—Michael Bourrett (Dystel & Goderich)

"A dream client is someone who writes wonderfully, understands promotion and knows how to build a tribe, always makes a deadline, is gracious with critique and direction, and is kind, grateful, smart, and makes me laugh."

—Rachelle Gardner (Books and Such Literary)

"Respect my time. Don't expect me to constantly call if there's no news to report. Trust that I know what I'm doing, and don't take the advice of writers at conferences or in your writing groups over mine. Have realistic expectations; don't expect me to drop everything and read your manuscript (a manuscript that took you a year or two to write) immediately. Understand that publishing moves slowly at times and I'm just as frustrated as you are if we have to wait for a check, a contract, or a response to a submitted manuscript."

—Jennifer De Chiara (Jennifer De Chiara Literary)

"A dream client is one whose talent continually surprises me, and my belief in it is what keeps me on my toes to make sure I'm doing right by his or her work."

—Brian DeFiore (DeFiore and Company)

"The best writers I work with are flexible and adaptable."

—Carly Watters (P.S. Literary Agency)

"Here are my dream client attributes: a natural ability to write—and well, a good idea of how to build a platform, a good attitude, and perseverance."

—Dawn Frederick (Red Sofa Literary)

"(1) Figure out what the best form of communication will be. If you are a person who needs to talk things out on the phone, let your agent know this so he or she can either know to set time aside for you or let you know what to expect from them in terms of phone time. If you like to send e-mails, I suggest getting all of your questions queued up and sending one message instead of rapid-fire e-mails throughout the day. [Establishing how and when you communicate] can take some practice, so both sides need to exercise some patience. (2) Try not to take things personally. [W]hile there will certainly be room for creative and friendly conversations, at the end of the day, you are both in this for an end goal: to get published and make some money, yes? Keep an open mind when discussing everything such as ideas for future projects, edits, conversations with editors, and more. (3) Generate lots of ideas. And don't feel you need to execute each one before talking about it with your agent. Be inspired by the world around you, and write about what excites you the most. But also be open [to input], and [be] realistic about what ideas need to be fleshed out now as opposed to being shelved for later."

—J.L. Stermer (N.S. Bienstock)

"Be patient [and] flexible, and let your agent help you navigate what can be a long and winding road to publication and to future books. Try to remember it's a marathon and not a sprint."

—Stacey Glick (Dystel & Goderich)

WHAT HAPPENS NEXT: LETTING YOUR AGENT WORK

One of the first questions you need to ask an interested agent is "What changes do you think need to be made before we submit?" Once you sign a contract with an agent, the key first step is making any final changes to the manuscript so the agent can attempt to sell it. This is the time when you work through those changes and create a finished product the agent believes she can sell.

After the manuscript is finalized, your agent is ready to submit to editors who seek what you're writing. This is what agents do best. Pitching to editors is their forte, and it's why you sign with them in the first place, so don't butt in and evaluate their decisions at this juncture. Step away, and let your agent work.

Typically the agent pitches to various "ideal" editors first—those who can offer the most money and support, or individuals who may have a deep personal connection to the work. Following her contact of "top tier" editors, agents may also target "secondary" markets if the initial contacts pass on the book.

All this takes time. A lot of editors will reject the work outright, but concerning the rest of the submissions, no news is indeed good news. If an editor likes the book, he has to jump through several hurdles before a deal is offered to the author and agent. The acquiring editor will have to present it at an editorial board meeting, run it by marketing, create a profit and loss estimate sheet, and get everything signed off by some of the highest bosses at the company. This is a not a quick process. So the truth is that to get a book deal, you don't just need one yes from an editor—you actually need several yes responses from key people who review it over the course of weeks or months.

"Everything takes longer than one expects, including the time from final delivery [of a finished manuscript to the publisher] until it's published. Once delivered, it can be hard to move on to the next project, but that's the best thing to do

193

if you haven't already begun doing so. I do not recommend [immediately] working on a prequel, sequel, or companion book, as the sale of one is too dependent on the success of the prior project. It's better to move on to a separate, stand-alone project, especially when early in one's career."

—Marcia Wernick (Wernick & Pratt Agency)

Different agents will have different styles of keeping writers abreast of happenings—this is why discussing communication style is so critical when signing with an agent—but you should always be able to get a status update if you occasionally ask for one—such as potential markets considering the work, as well as those that have formally rejected the book already. This stage of the process—the agent's submissions—has very little to do with the writer, and this is a great time to focus all your efforts on writing your next project or building your platform.

As the submission process continues, one of two things may happen: (1) Your book may hit some walls (i.e., lots of rejections), and the agent will touch base with you to regroup and discuss next steps moving forward, or (2) the book will attract the interest of one or more publishers as a deal comes closer to fruition.

If your book is not attracting interest from editors, your agent may suggest the submission process temporarily stall so changes can be made to the manuscript in an effort to make it more attractive to publishers. It's a time to evaluate your status and discuss next steps, whether that means a major overhaul of the book/proposal or abandoning the project and starting anew on another.

If the fortunate, opposite situation happens—interest does manifest for your novel or nonfiction book—three different things may happen, none of which are a bad thing.

1. **A PREEMPT.** This happens when your agent is still in the thick of submitting to editors and gauging responses. An editor will receive the book and like it so much that he contacts your agent and makes an offer right then and there. Because you and your agent

have yet to hear replies from many editors, this offer is called a "preempt"—it is designed to stop the submission process in its tracks. If an editor offers a preempt, it is a clear sign of passion for the project and can lead to a quick deal for all parties. Such an offer is rare. And while preempts are a sign of enthusiasm, they should be scrutinized and evaluated just like any other deal offer.

2. **AN AUCTION.** This occurs when two or more publishing houses want to buy the book, and thus your agent fields a bidding war during a particular day—until someone makes a winning bid that is not beaten. Publishers bid not only with money but also with promises of marketing support as well as possible offers to buy multiple books rather than just one. Auctions are rare but ideal. In such a bidding war, the competition drives up how much money you can make for an advance. In fact, editors are like agents in that they can smell blood in the water. Just as a writer's ability to get an offer of representation can draw quick interest from other agents considering the work, an agent's ability to secure a book deal can draw quick interest from other editors looking over the book.

3. **A NORMAL OFFER.** This is simply when an editor makes you an offer for the book—without the fanfare of a preempt or a bidding war with others. Most times, finding a publisher happens this way—including the long series of yeses throughout the company that we talked about earlier. At the heart of the process, though, is an editor who feels a deep connection with the work.

There are several major items that your agent and the editor must agree on before a deal is made. These are called "deal points" and involve things such as how much money you'll be paid up front and what rights to the material you're selling away. Once these crucial points are ironed out, the deal is, in all probability, going to happen. This is when your agent will call and tell you to finally pop open the champagne.

And although you can personally celebrate in this moment of happiness, it's wise to keep the good news under wraps for now. Yes, if your agent says the deal is good, then there is an overwhelming chance it's all said and done. But no contract has been signed yet, and anything can happen. Several years ago, my agent told me to pop the champagne on a book deal, and I did just that. (It was delicious.) But in the weeks to come, an unexpected disagreement concerning royalty rates in the contract shut down the negotiation process and the deal fell through. I was told this doesn't happen 95 percent of the time, but evidently this deal just fell in that 5 percent. For months, relatives and co-workers were asking me when the book would be out, only to hear my sheepish reply that there would be no book.

Besides running the risk of counting your chickens before they've hatched, if you celebrate too early and tell the whole world via Facebook, somebody could try to beat you to the punch. This is a much more common problem for nonfiction authors than novelists. Let's say you come up with a unique hook for your nonfiction book—such as the history of salt or a memoir "written" by God (both of these are real books), somebody can see that concept posted online and self-publish a book in an attempt to beat you to the punch. While nonfiction authors cannot completely prevent this type of idea theft, they can do themselves favors by not spreading the word until the book's marketing plan begins—perhaps at six months prior to its release.

MEETING YOUR EDITOR

Since an agent's job is to submit your book to all the editors she feels are a good fit for the work, chances are she's met these editors personally at least once, if not many times. That's what agents do—get to know editors. So if one of these editors makes an offer, your agent should be able to quickly give you the lowdown on the editor and what he's known for. In fact, there is a good probability your agent has sold to this editor before and can explain the process of how their previous collaboration transpired.

This is also when your agent will explain all the ideas and concerns that the editor has brought to the table. Before you say yes to the deal, it's important that you're completely aware of what you will get—i.e., money— and what you will give up—i.e., rights you're selling away. But it's also important to understand how the editor wants to change the work during his editorial process. Perhaps he wants to trim 10 percent of the book. Or perhaps he wants you to eliminate a subplot. You must be A-OK with these changes before signing any paperwork.

The reason you should be completely aware and comfortable with any suggested changes is this: Once you sign the contract and Publishing House XYZ is now paying you money for your book, *they* are in charge. They have purchased your material and therefore have the final say. Don't panic: Your opinion will factor in during the editing process. After all, you created the work and will have valuable thoughts on any changes to the story as well as other elements such as the cover and marketing ideas. A good editor will welcome your suggestions and start lines of dialogue on points that need to be ironed out. But when push comes to shove, remember who makes the final decision and who holds the purse strings.

Ideally your experience working with an editor will be pleasant, but that's less likely to happen if every little change to the manuscript generates an argument for you. Keeping a positive relationship is good for your future, too—you want to sell another book to this publishing house and work with the editor again. So keep the future in mind throughout the process, and remember that many writers praise editors after the fact for making their books stronger.

To keep your relationship with your editor positive, voice your concerns and frustrations to your agent first. Make your rep your sounding board and go-between. A good agent can help talk you down from ledges and explain why an editor's idea or opinion is actually not a bad thing and that it will help with the finished product. And if you have a legitimate problem with something the publishing house proposes (such as an unwise change to your title), it's better to let the agent bring up these thoughts with the editor. Remember, an agent, not you, should play bad cop. It's too important for an editor to have a good opinion of you so you'll work together again.

FOUR SIGNS OF AN UNHEALTHY AGENT-AUTHOR RELATIONSHIP

No author I know who signs with an agent wants that partnership to end. But, sadly, things do break down sometimes. Here are four signs that your agent-author relationship has turned sour.

1. **LACK OF COMMUNICATION FROM THE AGENT.** This is the big one. Most agents will respond to your e-mails within forty-eight hours, if not much quicker. But if you're e-mailing your agent and repeatedly getting nada in return, that's a bad sign. It means that your agent no longer considers you important enough to communicate with or she is simply avoiding you—or she doesn't know how to prioritize her time. A serious lack of communication is a large problem and one of the first signs of a sinking ship.

2. **DISAGREEMENT ON BIG ISSUES IN YOUR WRITING CAREER.** You and your agent should be on the same page concerning what you write and your career goals. Sometimes an agent sees an opening for you in another area and wants to guide you in that direction. You may take this change of direction easily, or you may not. If you feel uneasy writing what your agent wants you to write— whether it's a completely different type of book or the suggestion to change the age of your main character from thirty-three to sixty-three—then that's another red flag.

3. **DREADING TALKING WITH ONE ANOTHER.** Personally, I always look forward to my agent's phone calls. Why? Because she only calls with *news*, and news is welcome. Even bad news is welcome, because it gives us answers and closure, and helps us move on and decide the proper next step. So if you don't look forward to your agent's calls or she always acts put out when you get her on the phone, that's bad. This partnership is fueled by enthusiasm, and dread is the opposite of enthusiasm.

4. **A MAJOR DIFFERENCE OF OPINION ON AN OFFERED DEAL.** An agent's job is to get you a book deal. But, oddly enough, sometimes a deal offer can be a bad thing and lead to arguments between you and your agent. An agent is likely to be excited about her hard work paying off with a deal offer, but the deal may not be quite what you expected. All of the following scenarios are very plausible: (1) The offer comes from XYZ Publisher, but you've heard negative things about that house from writer friends. (2) The of-

fer for your nonfiction proposal was much lower than hoped, and you now feel like writing the rest of the book will not be financially worthwhile. (3) A publisher offers you a healthy deal, but they, in fact, want to make your book the next edition of an existing novel series and take your name off the book. (4) The publisher wants to release your book but only as an e-book at first, with print copies being discussed only after certain sales figures are reached. If your agent is pushing you hard to take the deal but your gut tells you no, that's never a good situation to be in.

So what happens if you feel like your efforts together have taken a downward turn? At that point, it's time to compose an honest e-mail expressing your concerns. Make sure you don't get upset or point fingers. Just calmly express what's on your mind. It's an invitation for the agent to write back and tell you what's frustrating her. You both have nothing to lose at this point, and it's time to stop holding back and express your true thoughts—albeit politely.

Ideally the open conversation will illuminate some issues or ideas you two didn't understand before. Then you can use it as a jumping-off point for getting your relationship—and your career—back on track.

Conversely, the conversation may confirm your fears that the match is not a true match and it's time to move on. The most common problem you are likely to address is a disagreement about how to move forward. If you feel very strongly about one course of action but your agent does not—like if you want to start writing picture books exclusively, while your agent says you need to stick to your bread-and-butter mystery books—there's not much you can do.

In the worst case, the agent may not even choose to reply to this e-mail. If that happens, it's time to pull up the anchor and sail on. You can then send a follow-up e-mail requesting the termination of your partnership, effective in however many days as set forth by your contract. Thank her for her time and hard work, and start drafting a new query letter to begin your agent search anew.

Keep in mind that if you want to find another rep who might be a better fit for your style, you should cut ties with your current agent before doing any new querying. It's disrespectful to both agents if you talk representation with new agents before formally terminating your current contract.

HOW MONEY AND PAYMENTS WORK: YOUR QUESTIONS ANSWERED

Let's put aside those end-times scenarios and focus on the good stuff: money. If you're going to wheel and deal with literary agents and editors, you'll end up spending more time than you'd like discussing rights, contracts, advances, royalties and a whole lot of other ~~boring~~ important stuff. This is a boundless topic, so here I'll address the most common questions regarding how the payment process works when you sell a book.

> *"Don't become a writer to get rich; it may happen, but it's a long road to getting there and most of the 'riches' come in other forms. Write because you feel you can't do anything else, because there are stories inside you that need to find their way out."*
>
> —Melissa Sarver (Folio Literary)

How do writers make money?

You sign a contract with a publisher. In exchange for signing over the North American and English-language print rights to your book and possibly other rights as well, you are paid one of three ways.

1. **FLAT FEE:** a set amount of money up front that's yours to keep. The amount does not change no matter how well the book sells. For example, if your flat fee is $10,000, the amount remains the same whether the book sells ten copies or ten million.
2. **ROYALTIES:** a small amount paid to you for every book sold.

3. **ADVANCE AGAINST ROYALTIES**: a sum of money up front to you with the promise of more (royalties) should the book sell well.

Which of the three methods above is most desirable?

An advance against royalties is probably the most desirable, and it is by far the most common. It's like you get both a flat fee and royalties combined. Let me explain exactly how an advance against royalties works. For this example, I'll keep it real simple. Let's say the publishing house offers you an advance of $30,000 and royalties of $3/book.

Note that the up-front advance of $30,000 is not *in addition* to royalties but rather *part* of royalties—meaning they've given you royalties for the first ten thousand books (times $3/book) up front. Since they've already paid you the royalties of the first ten thousand books, you will not start actually making an additional $3/book until you sell copy 10,001. The royalty possibilities are essentially endless. You can make $3/book forever as long as new copies keep selling in bookstores and online.

What if my book bombs? Do they get the money back?

No. Any up-front money—a flat fee or advance—is yours to keep no matter what. But you're on to something here with that question. If your book tanks and the project is a financial failure, you've created a huge hurdle to get over when you want to sell another book.

Yes, a huge advance means a large sum of guaranteed money (sweet), but a small advance means more reasonable expectations for you to meet and a greater chance for your book to be profitable, making you "a valuable author" in a publisher's eyes and more likely to get one or more book deals moving forward.

How much are royalties per book?

Totally depends on the cost of the book, your contract, and how much it is to produce copies of the work. If you write a hardback novel, you may get $3/book. If you write niche nonfiction, it's probably more like $1/book. And keep in mind that if you write with a co-writer or an illustrator, that royalty is likely cut in half.

How much money can authors expect from their first advance?

This is the big question that never gets answered. The reason it never gets answered is not because editors are being coy but rather because *there is no answer.* The amount of your advanced payment is, for the most part, dependent on how many books the editor has projected you will definitely sell. It also depends on the book's genre/category, the size of the house, the scope of the deal, your platform, your agent's skill, and much more. There are just as many $3,000 deals going on in a day as there are $100,000 deals. *That's* why there is no answer. No one wants to throw a figure out there that is interpreted as fact.

Hope for money, but write because you *love it.* It's not healthy to come in with a particular financial expectation. Three grand may sound like peanuts, but it can be reality. You should not be in the writing business for the money. The second you say, "I will not sell my book for anything less than [X]," you're backing yourself into a corner. Perhaps you're an engineer making $60/hour at your full-time job. If you decide to write a book on engineering, there is virtually no chance that the work you put into that project (writing, pitching, marketing) will amount to $60/hour. Know this going in so that both you and the agent aren't disappointed.

Are there any trends in money and advances these days?

Yes. Sadly, advances are trending down slowly. For example, a book that would have garnered you a $15,000 advance ten years ago may only gain about 50–60 percent of that total today. But the good news is that if your book sells well, there's still plenty of money to be made on the back end with royalties. And with e-book publishers and partner publishers, there are more avenues than ever to sell in the first place—so don't listen to anyone who says it's all gloom out there.

When do you receive the money after you sign your contract?

It depends, but that money is usually split into multiple payments. For example, if you sign a deal for $12,000, you may get $4,000 upon signing the contract, then another third upon completion of editing or writing the project, then the final third when the book is released.

Do writers get the checks from the publisher?

Typically, no. In my case, the check gets sent to my literary agent, who cashes it. She is then required to, within ten days, send me a check for 85 percent of the original amount. An agent's standard commission is 15 percent of all monies made off the book. (The agent sends you a 1099 at the end of the year, so you can pay taxes.) Oh, and be aware that the checks from the publisher don't come quickly. If I sell copies of my humor books in January, the royalty check doesn't land until November usually. So patience is key.

How do I make sure that I'm getting paid properly?

I'm honestly not sure, and that's why I encourage you to find a literary agent. It's the agent's responsibility to be in touch with the editor and accounting department to make sure the royalty statements (payments) accurately reflect proper totals that take into account sales, returns, foreign-territory sales, and film rights.

Do you make money for selling foreign rights and film rights?

Traditionally, yes—as long as you don't have an unfortunate contract that deems otherwise. If a production studio wants to buy your film rights, they have to pay you—and that isn't cheap, either. They will likely *option* your book, meaning that they buy the film rights temporarily (for example, one year) in exchange for a limited amount of money. And a film company can certainly continue to option the book repeatedly year after year if they're making progress and don't want to let the property go. And that's good financial news for you!

For every foreign territory (country) that you sell to where the book requires a translation, that's more money. Advances and royalties work the same way in other countries: You get a small lump sum of cash (an advance) for each territory, with the possibility of more money (royalties) should the book sell well. If the book sells in ten territories, that's a great way to make money off a project. Plus it's pretty darn cool to see the different covers of your book with the title in different languages.

When multiple publishing houses are interested in your work, should you just go with the highest bidder?

Not necessarily. Money will play a big, big role in the selling of the book—but there is more to consider. Are they promising a thorough marketing and publicity plan? Do they seem excited about the book? What rights are they asking for in exchange for that money? Do they design and produce beautiful books? Do they have a history of keeping their books in print for years and still promoting them down the road? Do they publish ten books a year or four hundred, and how will that play out in how your book is handled? All these questions factor in big time. In my opinion, it's better to take a $10,000 deal with a house that loves the book and will push it than a house that offers double the advance but not a whole lot of love. It's love and enthusiasm for a book that will give it the best possible chance to sell well.

"An offer in your pocket is always better than none," says Laura Langlie, founder of the Laura Langlie Agency. "Certainly, if an agent feels she can demand more for a book, she should hold out; however, usually the editor who makes the first offer is the most enthusiastic and thoroughly understands the book and may turn out to be the best editor and in-house advocate for that book. The most money is not necessarily the best deal for an author. That enthusiasm, commitment, and support from all divisions within a publishing house often means more than those dollars in your bank account. An agent's experience regarding what editors are looking to buy, what publishers are currently paying, and what the marketplace is like should lead that agent to advise her client regarding whether or not an offer on the table is the best (whatever its true meaning) that can be expected."

You may find yourself taking a deal you didn't expect to take—such as with an e-book-only publisher—because it's simply what makes the most sense for your book and your career. There are many factors that will go into this decision when it comes. Your agent will guide you through every step as your dream grows and changes, and as your book makes its way into print.

CHAPTER FIFTEEN

FINAL ADVICE FROM AGENTS

Literary agents have great advice for writers. Whenever I interview an agent, I close with this question: "Is there any other piece of advice you'd like to mention?" Here are agents' honest, earnest, encouraging answers to that question. Use their insights to push and inspire you as you begin your journey to getting a literary agent.

> *"Read and share. I think it is critical to really read and analyze published books that are similar to what you want to write and really study them to see how the successful authors are doing it. How do the successful authors in your area develop characters? Give backstory? Create tension? Keep pacing up? POV? Voice? Develop setting?"*
>
> —Jill Marsal (Marsal Lyon Literary Agency)

> *"One of the things I stress is persistence. When submitting query letters, persistence is key, but authors must be smart about their approach as well. Make sure you have a well-curated list of agents you are going to query. Make sure they are truly a good fit for you. Keep meticulous notes during the process. And if you get any constructive criticism, do not be defensive*

and shrug it off—see if you can use it to make your pitch better. So many people give up after a few rejections. Keep the process moving by honing your letter as well as your manuscript or book proposal. And stay positive! This is a hard one, I know, but bitter and frustrated authors send out that vibe and I can always sense it—in person and even in query letters. You are selling your project, so sell it with a smile on your face."

—J.L. Stermer (N.S. Bienstock)

"Be well-read in your genre and know the market. Don't give up! In particular, don't get stuck on one project. Sometimes you need to put a book aside and start something new."

—Jessica Alvarez (BookEnds)

"The best advice I can give to an aspiring author is to get serious about your career. It's more than a hobby. You have to be focused and educated. Join writers' organizations or a critique group. Read, read, read, and read some more in the genre you want to write in, and search the Web on the proper way to format a manuscript and query an agent way before you start submitting. Our agency gets three hundred submissions a week. In order to stand out, your query letter has to be beyond reproach, and when we ask for sample pages, they need to be in A+ shape. If you've done your homework, you will be successful."

—Deidre Knight (The Knight Agency)

"The act of writing may be solitary, but improving your craft isn't accomplished in isolation. Make the most of your writing resources—attend conferences, take part in the power of writing communities, embrace professional feedback and critiques of your work, and let your ego down long enough to funnel everything into your writing."

—Kimiko Nakamura (Dee Mura Literary)

"Trust yourself. Trust your instincts."

—Katie Shea Boutillier (Donald Maass Literary Agency)

"If I had to name five things I'd look for in a prospective writer, they would be:
- *Professionalism—ability to divorce your ego as much as possible from the process*
- *Sufficient understanding of books and the book market to know whether your idea works as a book-length narrative as opposed to a magazine article or short story*
- *Creativity and understanding of narrative form*
- *Willingness and ability to take editorial direction*
- *Willingness to do whatever work is necessary to make the work saleable"*

—Deborah Grosvenor (Grosvenor Literary Agency)

"It might seem obvious, but one of the most important things a writer can do is just write. *It's like working any muscle. The more you use it, the stronger it is going to get. Not everyone has the talent or timing or luck to be a best-selling author, but the ones who find the most success are often the ones who are able to write well consistently and learn and grow. To be prolific and successful, you have to write!"*

—Stacey Glick (Dystel & Goderich)

"Woody Allen said 80 percent of success is just showing up. It's different for writers. Eighty percent of success for a writer is working hard. You can't underestimate how important it is to put in the hours. Read, write, study the business. Repeat. Day after day."

—Howard Yoon (Ross Yoon Literary)

"Pursue every opportunity to improve your craft, and be patient. Likely your first project won't be 'the one,' but it might be your third (or tenth) manuscript where you find your voice and write the book you were meant to write. Don't give up!"

—Sara Sciuto (Full Circle Literary)

"Read as much as you can, especially in the genre you are writing in. You need to know your market and your competition as well as what has already been done and what new things you can bring to the table. Do not just write about what you know, because that can often be boring. Write the book you want to read; then figure out how to pitch it when you finish writing. Join a critique group so you are not writing in a vacuum. Keep revising your manuscript until it is in the best possible shape before you start querying agents. Be courteous in your dealing[s] with agents, as we have very good memories and will remember you when you contact us again. Be patient, be realistic, but be persistent."

—Sandy Lu (L. Perkins Agency)

"(1) Don't quit your day job! With advances getting smaller as the publishing industry doldrums continue, most authors should not expect to make a living solely by their writing. (2) Learn how to market yourself and create a platform—a website, a blog, write a column for a newspaper, etc. Publishers need authors who can bring a built-in audience to their books. (3) Write about things people want to read. Sounds simple, doesn't it? (4) I don't believe in writer's block. If you write every day, even if it's a page of crap, the very act of writing (or typing) will begin to get the creative juices flowing. So sit your butt down in the chair and start hammering away at those keys. Books don't write themselves."

—Doug Grad (Doug Grad Literary Agency)

"Don't take rejection personally."

—David Dunton (Harvey Klinger, Inc.)

"Do it for yourself. Write because it's your passion, you need to do it, and you have something to say. Your ultimate goal should be to be the very best writer you can be, not simply to get published. Fame and money shouldn't be your goals; you shouldn't be talking about a movie deal or why you think your book would make a great reality show. It's not about perspiration but inspiration. Just because you've worked hard on a manuscript doesn't mean that it should be published."

—Jennifer De Chiara (Jennifer De Chiara Literary)

"Don't give up. Don't ever give up. Any dream is achievable if you work hard enough."

—Nicole Resciniti (The Seymour Agency)

"Stay true to yourself. Be aware of the conventions of your genre, but don't try and write something because it's trendy. If your heart's not in it, it's going to feel forced. If you don't write something that excites you—and if you don't write from the heart—you're not going to win anybody over."

—Rachael Dugas (Talcott Notch Literary Services)

"If you pitch a project to me (or another agent) and my response is something along the lines of 'this isn't right for me,' remember this: It isn't personal. I'm not attacking you as a person, and I'm not even attacking your writing. There are plenty of books out there that I love but that I also know I wouldn't be the right agent for. More important than finding an agent is finding the right agent."

—Brooks Sherman (The Bent Agency)

"If an agent passes on your manuscript but tells you they would love to look at a revision, they mean it! They think you have talent and they want to see more from you. However, the flip side of a request like this is that they probably feel there is still a lot

of work to be done before they could successfully market your project to editors. Give yourself the greatest chance by always sending agents your very best work."

—Shira Hoffman (McIntosh & Otis, Inc.)

"Watch what you say online. I know it seems like common sense, but you wouldn't believe the number of people who blog, tweet, or post inappropriate things online. It's better to just not do it; if you post and delete, it's still archived. An online presence is an agent's or editor's first impression of you—make it a good one."

—Kathleen Ortiz (New Leaf Literary and Media)

"Spend a lot of time writing your query letter. Read a book about it; take a class on it; do whatever it takes. Your query letter is your first impression—don't make it your last. You also want to take a long, hard look at your first twenty pages. Cut out every sentence, paragraph, or word that is extraneous; show no mercy, because your readers certainly won't. And lastly, don't be afraid to quit and try something different. Not every project is going to be a winner, and you're not going to make it a bestseller by willing it to be so. Besides, if you don't sincerely believe that your next book will be better than your last, then being a professional writer is probably not going to work out for you anyway."

—Evan Gregory (Ethan Ellenberg Literary Agency)

"Research! There's an overwhelming amount of information out there on publishing."

—Sara D'Emic (formerly of Talcott Notch Literary Services)

"Writing is rewriting—make your work the best it can be before you try to market."

—Kimberley Cameron (Kimberley Cameron & Associates)

"Start marketing yourself right now."

—Bree Ogden (D4EO Literary)

"Join a writing group. There are few things more valuable to a writer than an honest and insightful reader. Family and friends are often too biased to give real criticism. A writing group can help give you a broader perspective on your manuscript, help you see what's working and what's not—all while providing support and encouragement. Even when the group isn't meeting, the process of editing each other's books will have made you better at self-editing."

—Adam Schear (DeFiore and Company)

"It's always tempting to write something that seems trendy. Much of this business is about the selling aspect, so writers often think that if they write what publishers seem to be publishing or what seems to be appearing on bestseller lists, then they have a greater chance of getting a contract—but I honestly don't think it's the wisest way to go. Sure, a writer needs to be aware of what's out there, both so you're not reinventing the wheel (i.e., writing a book that's essentially already been published) [and] so you know how to position your book—but you really need to write what you write best. This means if you've never written for the YA market and have little sense of that audience, then starting now probably doesn't make sense, nor for that matter does reinventing yourself as a political writer if you don't already have a column or blog that's well known in that arena. You're not likely to 'fool' publishers simply by trying to do what's hot."

—Felicia Eth (Felicia Eth Literary Representation)

"I think there is a gap between what writers think is 'market ready' and what an agent or editor does. Without getting professional feedback, it's difficult to bridge that gap. If you want to be traditionally published, use freelance book editors, preferably who have industry experience, to polish your work before approach-

ing an agent or editor. Freelance editors can be costly, but I think they save writers time and money in the long run."

—Elizabeth Kracht (Kimberley Cameron & Associates)

"Great writers also need to be great readers. To stay on top of the market, read as many recently published books in your genre as you can."

—Molly Jaffa (Folio Literary Management)

"Follow your dreams. Keep your fingers crossed—and try to have fun."

—Linda Epstein (Jennifer De Chiara Literary Agency)

"I definitely see too many people trying to be something else. I used to make the mistake of listing Roald Dahl as one of my favorite writers from my childhood, but I've found that just inspires a bunch of Dahl knockoffs. And trust me; it's tough to imitate the greats. I get far too many emulations of Dahl, Snicket, Rowling, and whatever else has worked in the past. It's one thing to aspire to greatness; it's another to imitate it. I want people who can appeal to me in the same way as successful writers of yore, with a style that's their own. I see too few writers willing to take chances."

—Chris Richman (formerly of Upstart Crow Literary)

"Be patient. If you are looking for instant gratification, our industry is going to disappoint you."

—Cameron McClure (Donald Maass Literary Agency)

"I think authors can drive themselves crazy worrying about 'marketability.' I don't think new fiction authors are going to connect

with readers unless they write about something that's meaningful to them. Writing for the market usually doesn't work. To me, the most important thing when looking at a debut novel that doesn't fall into an obvious commercial genre is how well and deeply it engages the reader."

—Alex Glass (Glass Literary)

"Revise, revise, revise. And read what is out there and doing well. You really do have to know your market."

—Elisabeth Weed (Weed Literary)

"My best piece of advice for writers is to keep writing. The more a writer writes, the better his or her skill becomes. And I also find that when an author derives joy from whatever he or she is writing, that joy comes through in the writing. So try to enjoy it, and that pleasure might speak directly to your readers."

—Faye Bender (Faye Bender Literary Agency)

CONCLUSION

Now you're *ready.*

You're ready to take on the submission process and tackle the goal of finding a literary agent head-on. But just because you soaked up the info in this book doesn't mean you can stop learning. Remember that the publishing industry is slowly evolving: Stay abreast of changes so you can always be aware of possible opportunities and changes that affect agents, your writing career, and your books.

And no matter what you write, no matter how many times you stumble along the way, you must never give up. As writers who seek to better our craft and knowledge, *we get better with time*—and that is an encouraging thought.

Good luck moving forward! Please stay in touch with me throughout your journey. I love to hear from my readers. Find me at Chucksambuchino. com, on Twitter at @chucksambuchino, or on Facebook.

GLOSSARY

AND RESOURCES

GLOSSARY OF PUBLISHING TERMS

ACQUISITIONS EDITOR. The person responsible for originating and/or acquiring new publishing projects (i.e., books). Your agent will pitch your books to acquisitions editors.

ADAPTATION. The process of rewriting a composition (novel, story, film, article, play) into a form suitable for some other medium, such as television or the stage.

ADVANCE. Money a publisher pays a writer prior to book publication, usually paid in installments such as one-half upon signing the contract and one-half upon delivery of the complete, satisfactory manuscript. An advance is paid against the royalty money to be earned by the book. Agents take their percentage off the top of the advance as well as from the royalties earned.

APP (APPLICATION). A computer program downloaded onto electronic devices—such as laptops, phones, or e-readers—that serves a specific purpose. Apps are designed to be user-friendly alternatives to doing the same task through an Internet window.

AUCTION. Multiple publishers sometimes bid for the acquisition of a book manuscript with excellent sales prospects. The bids are for the amount of the author's advance, advertising and promotional expenses, royalty percentage, etc. Auctions are conducted by agents.

AUTHOR BIO. A brief summary about the writer that includes work experience, educational experience, previous publishing history (if applicable), and social media links where interested individuals can learn more about the author.

AUTHOR COPIES. An author usually receives about ten free copies of his hardcover book from the publisher; he'll get more from a paperback firm. He can obtain additional copies at a price that has been reduced by an author's discount (usually 50 percent of the retail price).

BACKLIST. A publisher's list of books that were not published during the current season but that are still in print.

BACKSTORY. The history of what has happened before the action in your story takes place; events that affect a character's current behavior.

BLURB. The copy on paperback-book covers or hardcover-book dust jackets, either promoting the book and the author or featuring testimonials from book reviewers or well-known people in the book's field.

BOOK PROPOSAL. A document, usually twelve to fifty pages in length, which lays out the concept and marketing ideas for a nonfiction book. For writers selling nonfiction, a book proposal is their key selling tool.

CLIPS. These are samples from newspapers, websites, or magazines of your published work. Also called "tear sheets," though that term is only used when the clips you send are physical copies.

CLOSED TO SUBMISSIONS. A phrase used by agents when they are currently not accepting queries of any kind from new writers.

CONFLICT. A prime ingredient of fiction that usually represents some obstacle to a character's (i.e., the protagonist's) goals.

COPYEDITING. Editing of a manuscript for writing style, grammar, punctuation, and factual accuracy.

COPYRIGHT. A means to protect an author's work. A copyright is a proprietary right designed to give the creator of a work the power to control that work's reproduction, distribution, and public display or performance, as well as its adaptation to other forms. All written works are copyrighted the moment they are created.

DEAL MEMO. The memorandum of agreement between a publisher and author that precedes the actual contract and includes important issues such as royalty, advance, rights, distribution, and option clauses.

DIALOGUE. An essential element of fiction. Dialogue consists of conversations between two or more people and can be used heavily or sparsely.

E-BOOK. A book in electronic form—read on reading devices such as a computer, Nook, iPad, or Kindle.

ENHANCED E-BOOK. An e-book that has added features and interactive elements, such as embedded videos, hyperlinks to articles, supplemental materials, updated images, and more.

ELECTRONIC RIGHTS (ALSO CALLED DIGITAL RIGHTS). Rights dealing with electronic/multimedia formats (the Internet, digital downloads, CD-ROMs, electronic magazines).

EXCLUSIVE. An agreement, usually for a set period of time such as one month, guaranteeing that an agent or editor is the only one looking at a particular manuscript.

FILM RIGHTS. May be sold or optioned by the agent or author to a person in the film industry, enabling the book to be made into a movie.

FOREIGN RIGHTS. Translation or reprint rights to be sold abroad.

FOREIGN-RIGHTS AGENT. An agent who sells book rights to a country other than the first book agent's country. Typically, an author surrenders a 20 percent commission to his agents for any foreign rights sales, as opposed to the standard 15 percent commission.

GENRE. Refers to either a general classification of writing, such as a novel, poem, or short story, or to the categories within those classifications, such as romance, mystery, or fantasy.

GHOSTWRITING. A writer puts into literary form the words, ideas, or knowledge of another person under that person's name. Some agents will pair ghostwriters with celebrities or experts.

HIGH CONCEPT. A story idea easily expressed in a one-line description.

HOOK. Aspect of the work that sets it apart from others and draws in the reader.

IMPRINT. The name applied to a publisher's specific line of books.

IRC (INTERNATIONAL REPLY COUPON). Buy this at a post office to enclose with material sent outside the country to cover the cost of return postage. The recipient exchanges the coupon for stamps in her country.

ISBN (INTERNATIONAL STANDARD BOOK NUMBER). ISBN is a tool used for both ordering and cataloging purposes as well as a means for tracking the sales history of a particular book.

LIBEL. A form of defamation or injury to a person's name or reputation. Written or published defamation is called "libel," whereas spoken defamation is known as "slander."

LOG LINE. A one-sentence plot description.

MIDLIST. Those titles on a publisher's list expected to have limited sales. Midlist books are mainstream, not literary, scholarly, or genre.

NOVELIZATION. A novel created from the script of a popular movie and published in paperback. Also called a movie tie-in.

NOVELLA. A short novel or long short story, usually 20,000 to 50,000 words. Also called a novelette.

ONE-TIME RIGHTS. This right allows a short story or portions of a fiction or nonfiction book to be published again without violating the contract.

OPTION. The act of a producer buying film rights to a book for a limited period of time (usually six months or one year) rather than purchasing said rights in full. A book can be optioned multiple times by different production companies.

OPTION CLAUSE. A contract clause giving a publisher the right to publish an author's next book. This is a very important term that your agent will negotiate with the publisher so as to give you, the author, the most avenues for selling future books.

OUT OF PRINT. A phrase describing books that no longer sell many print copies and are therefore not printed any longer. The definition of this term, as well as its role in contracts, is changing because of the fact that e-books are technically "in print" forever.

PLATFORM. A writer's speaking experience, interview skills, website, social media, and other abilities that help form a following of potential buyers for his book.

P.O.D. (PRINT ON DEMAND). A publisher that only creates copies of a book once it has been ordered, eliminating the cost of overstock and unused print copies.

PROOFREADING. Close reading and correction of a manuscript's typographical errors.

QUERY. A letter, usually around one page long, written to an agent or a potential market to elicit interest in a writer's work.

REFERRAL. When a writer passes on the name or work of another writer to his agent.

RELEASE. A document stating that your idea is original, that it has never been sold to anyone else, and that you are selling negotiated rights to the idea upon payment. Some agents may ask that you sign a release before they request pages and review your work.

REMAINDERS. Leftover stock of a book that the publisher believes will not sell at a cover price. Remainders are typically sold at a deep discount so the publisher can recoup some expenses and costs.

REPRINT RIGHTS. The right to republish a book after its initial printing.

ROYALTIES. A percentage of the retail price paid to the author for each copy of the book that is sold. Agents take their percentage from the royalties earned and from the author's advance.

SASE (SELF-ADDRESSED STAMPED ENVELOPE). One should be included with all mailed correspondence if you want a reply via mail. An alternative to this is a self-addressed, stamped postcard.

SERIAL RIGHTS. The right for a newspaper or magazine to publish sections of a manuscript.

SIMULTANEOUS SUBMISSION. The common practice of sending the same query or manuscript to several agents or publishers at the same time.

SLUSH PILE. A stack of unsolicited submissions in the office of an editor, agent, or publisher.

SUBSIDIARY RIGHTS. All rights other than book publishing rights included in a book publishing contract, such as paperback rights, book club rights, and movie rights. Part of an agent's job is to negotiate those rights and advise you on which to sell and which to keep.

SUSPENSE. The element of both fiction and some nonfiction that makes the reader uncertain about the outcome. Suspense can be created through almost any element of a story, including the title, characters, plot, time restrictions, and word choice.

SYNOPSIS. A brief summary of a story, novel, or play. Unlike a query letter or log line, a synopsis is a front-to-back explanation of the work—and will give away the story's ending.

TERMS. The agreed-upon financial provisions in a contract, whether between writer and agent or writer and editor.

TOC (TABLE OF CONTENTS). A listing at the beginning of a book indicating chapter titles and their corresponding page numbers. It can also include chapter descriptions.

TRANSLATION RIGHTS. Sold to a foreign agent or foreign publisher.

UNSOLICITED MANUSCRIPT. An unrequested full manuscript sent to an editor, agent, or publisher.

VET. Editorial term for submitting a book manuscript to an outside expert (such as a lawyer) for review before publication. Memoirs are frequently vetted to confirm factual accuracy before the book is published.

GLOSSARY OF GENRES AND CATEGORY DEFINITIONS

ACTION/ADVENTURE. A genre of fiction in which action is the key element, sometimes even overshadowing characters and theme. Note that these genre terms are rarely applied in the literary world and are used mostly to describe film.

AMISH FICTION. A newer genre of books that focuses on Amish characters and lifestyle—sometimes touching on the inspirational genre. Examples include *The Shunning* by Beverly Lewis and *The Choice* by Suzanne Woods Fisher.

AUTOBIOGRAPHY. An autobiography is a book-length account of a person's entire life written by the subject himself.

BIOGRAPHY. A biography is an account of a person's life (or the lives of a family or close-knit group) written by someone other than the subject. The work is set within the historical framework (i.e., the unique economic, social, and political conditions) existing during the subject's life.

BOARD BOOK. Also called "books for toddlers," board books are very simple texts that focus on elements like colors, numbers, and animals. They target children before they can read (ages one to four). They derive their name from the fact that most are printed on thick cardboard pages.

BOOK CLUB FICTION. See *mainstream fiction.*

CHAPTER BOOK. A category of children's books intended for intermediate readers, usually ages six to eleven. Chapter books are often the first step for children who have learned to read and are past picture books.

CHICK LIT. Stories that focus on female characters, with lighthearted, "breezy" themes of romance, careers, and, oftentimes, fashion and shopping. While chick lit peaked as a genre during the success of the television show *Sex and the City*, it is now considered a "challenging" genre to publish or market, and is usually pitched and marketed today as "light women's fiction."

CHRISTIAN LIVING. A category of books focused on self-help but with a Christian overview and tone. Christian living titles can be about parenting, marriage, family life, divorce, breast cancer, healing, health, faith journeys, spiritual challenges, leadership, and devotionals.

COMMERCIAL FICTION. Novels designed to appeal to a broad audience. Commercial fiction is a broad term that can mean different things to different agents, but it is typically used as a synonym for "genre fiction."

CREATIVE NONFICTION. See *narrative nonfiction*.

CRIME FICTION. An umbrella term used to classify stories where crime, police, private investigators, and police detectives are central to the plot.

DYSTOPIAN FICTION. Stories set in a bleak future where living conditions are harsh, usually because of an oppressive government or a change in world living conditions, such as from a nuclear disaster. Examples include The Hunger Games series and the Divergent series.

EROTICA. A form of literature dealing with the sexual aspects of love. Erotic content will typically include explicit descriptions of sexual acts.

FAMILY SAGA. A story that chronicles the lives of a family or a number of related or interconnected families over a period of time.

FANTASY. Stories set in invented worlds or in a legendary, mythic past that rely on outright invention or magic for conflict and setting. Examples include the Harry Potter series and *The Lord of the Rings*.

GENRE FICTION. An umbrella term that encompasses any of the so-called major genre categories of fiction, such as thriller, mystery, horror, romance, science fiction, and fantasy. If an agent explains she seeks genre fiction, it can be assumed she accepts all of the genre categories, but writers should still do their research, as sometimes agents may have a particular passion for one genre and not for another.

GRAPHIC NOVEL. A mix of novel and comics. A graphic novel contains comic-like drawings and captions—and can choose to deal with both everyday issues and more adventurous elements such as superheroes.

HISTORICAL FICTION. A story set in a recognizable period of history. In addition to telling the stories of ordinary people's lives, historical fiction may involve political or social events of the time.

HORROR. A story that aims to evoke some combination of fear, fascination, and revulsion in its readers—either through supernatural or psychological circumstances.

HOW-TO. A category of nonfiction book that offers the reader a description of how something can be accomplished. It includes both information and advice.

INSPIRATIONAL FICTION. An umbrella term that refers to stories and books with religious (usually Christian) content. Inspirational books can be overtly Christian in nature, or they can have simpler, subtler religious themes. Amish fiction is sometimes lumped into this category.

LGBT (LESBIAN/GAY/BISEXUAL/TRANSGENDER). These are stories where an openly LGBT character is central to the story, oftentimes the main character—though his or her sexuality may or may not be the main issue in the story. In recent years, *Q* has sometimes been added to the initials: LGBTQ—with the final letter meaning "questioning" and/or "queer."

LITERARY FICTION. A book in which style and technique are often as important as subject matter. In literary fiction, character is typically more important than plot, and the writer's voice and skill with words are both very essential. Literary fiction is a term often applied to novels that do not fall within a recognizable category such as romance or mystery.

MAGICAL REALISM. Stories set in our normal, realistic world that feature some element of magic that affects the plot. In film, Woody Allen's *Midnight in Paris* serves as an example. Stephen King's novel *The Green Mile* also fits this category.

MAINSTREAM FICTION. Sometimes called "book club fiction" by industry insiders, this term usually refers to nongenre stories that have mass appeal and transcend literary fiction readers.

MEMOIR. A first-person, true-life tale told by the author. Generally the term *memoir* is used for most life stories, whereas celebrities and politicians use *autobiography*. Memoir is typically the sole category of non-fiction that is treated like fiction in terms of submissions—in that the book should be complete before the writer queries agents.

MIDDLE-GRADE (MG). Books for children aged eight through twelve. These books are usually 20,000 to 55,000 words in length and deal with children getting involved in adventures or unusual situations. Because of the readers' ages, these titles typically avoid hot-button issues such as sex, drugs, alcohol, and abuse. Examples include the Diary of a Wimpy Kid series.

MISERY MEMOIR. An unofficial term used for memoirs that deal with loss, death, and tragedy. Agents often get stories like these, but few get published because most are written as catharsis for the writer rather than enjoyment for the reader.

MULTICULTURAL FICTION. Stories and novels in which many or all of the central characters are minorities African Americans, Hispanic, Jewish, First Peoples, or other. Sometimes called "ethnic fiction," multicultural fiction usually deals with a protagonist caught between two conflicting ways of life: mainstream American culture and ethnic heritage.

MYSTERY. A form of narration in which one or more elements remain unknown or unexplained until the end of the story. Subgenres include amateur sleuth, caper, cozy, heist, malice domestic, police procedural, and others.

NARRATIVE NONFICTION. Nonfiction stories that employ techniques used by novelists, such as character arc, the three-act structure, scenes, dialogue, and more. Examples: *Into the Wild, The Right Stuff, Seabiscuit.* While some agents will want to see a completed manuscript in a submission, most agents will instead request a nonfiction book proposal and sample chapters.

NEW ADULT FICTION. A newer genre of fiction featuring protagonists aged eighteen to twenty-six who grapple with the first major challenges of adulthood and maturity. This age range for protagonists used to be something of a "no man's land" for novels—too old for young adult fiction and too young for adult fiction. The category term came about as a means to classify these stories.

PARANORMAL FICTION. Stories that focus on invented dark elements that present danger in our world. This genre is very close to paranormal romance and urban fantasy. Examples include *Dracula* by Bram Stoker and the Sookie Stackhouse novels by Charlaine Harris.

PARANORMAL ROMANCE. See *urban fantasy* and *paranormal fiction.*

PICTURE BOOK. A type of book aimed at children aged three to eight that tells the story partially or entirely with artwork. Agents interested in selling to publishers of these books often handle both artists and writers.

POPULAR FICTION. See *genre fiction.*

REGIONAL FICTION. A book that's faithful to a particular geographic region and its people, and features their behavior, customs, speech, and history. Southern fiction is an example of a regional category.

ROMANCE. Stories that focus on a growing romantic love between two people and conclude with a happy ending. The story is told from the viewpoint of the heroine, and the relationship defines the central arc of the story. Subgenres include regency, historical, single-title, and more.

SCIENCE FICTION. Literature involving elements of science and technology as a basis for conflict or as the setting for a story. Examples include

Ender's Game by Orson Scott Card and *Dune* by Frank Herbert. Subgenres include cyberpunk, space operas, dystopian, and others.

TEXTBOOK. Books used in school classrooms at the elementary, high school, or college level.

THRILLER. Stories intended to arouse feelings of excitement, danger, action, and suspense. Works in this genre are highly sensational, usually focusing on illegal activities, international espionage, sex, and violence. Subgenres include techno-thrillers, legal thrillers, medical thrillers, military thrillers, and more.

TWEEN. A category of books that straddles the line between middle-grade fiction and young adult fiction. Though agents confirm this category's existence and some publishers specifically look for tween material, many bookstores lack a bookshelf for tween, and that is likely why the category remains small and somewhat under the radar.

UPMARKET FICTION. This term usually refers to women's fiction stories that have the ability to attract book club readers and even cross over to men. Examples include *The Help* by Kathryn Stockett and *My Sister's Keeper* by Jodi Picoult.

URBAN FANTASY. Stories set on Earth in a normal reality—but involving some kind of supernatural or fantastical element that enters the storyline, such as vampires or magician characters. (Many urban fantasy stories are called "paranormal romance" even though the two are technically different because some urban fantasy stories do not have a romantic element.) An example of this category is the Twilight series.

URBAN FICTION. Stories that focus on life in the inner city—usually featuring African American characters. Examples include *The Coldest Winter Ever* by Sister Souljah and *Flyy Girl* by Omar Tyree.

WESTERN. Stories set in the American West that center on classic characters and actions such as cowboys, ranching, gunfights, sprawling land, horses, Native Americans, and more. Though the genre term is usually associated with stories of the "Old West" that take place in the nineteenth century (*Lonesome Dove*), Western fiction can also cross with other genres. *Brokeback Mountain* could be considered a Western romance, the film *Near Dark* is an example of Western horror, and the comic book *Cowboys & Aliens* is Western science fiction.

WOMEN'S FICTION. Stories that center on a woman's emotional journey and do not lend themselves to any of the popular genres. Examples include *A Summer All Her Own* by Roseanne Keller and *Beautiful Day* by Elin Hilderbrand. When women's fiction has breakout potential, as well as the ability to attract male readers, it may be labeled "upmarket fiction."

YOUNG ADULT FICTION. The general classification of books written for ages twelve to eighteen. They run 40,000 to 90,000 words and include category novels: adventure, sports, paranormal, science fiction, fantasy, multicultural, mysteries, romance, etc. Young adult books typically feature a protagonist aged sixteen to eighteen and can address mature topics that real teens face.

LITERARY AGENT ROUNDUP

GENRE INSIGHTS, TIPS, AND DEFINITIONS

ON WRITER MISTAKES IN YOUNG ADULT
AND JUVENILE FICTION

"Bad children's writers don't think very highly of children—in a picture book, they go for cute instead of clever. In middle-grade fiction, they overexplain or dramatize a character's emotions so the reader is sure to 'get it.' And in young adult, they assume edgy only means sex and drugs, not the tightrope of teenagers' emotional lives."

—Quinlan Lee (formerly of Adams Literary)

"I've seen a lot of young adult novels lately set in the 1980s or 1990s that don't need to be; I think it is because this is when the writers remember being teenagers. However, it is important to remember that the 1990s are historical fiction to today's readers, and if the story can work at all set in the present, it probably should be."

—Lauren MacLeod (The Strothman Agency)

"For those young adult projects written in first person, watch that your characters aren't too 'voice-y' and don't go off on stream-of-consciousness tangents that slow the pace. Also, be sure your word count and the ages of your characters are appropriate for the genre (young adult readers read up in age). Avoid one-dimensional storytelling; employ subplots."

—Elizabeth Kracht (Kimberley Cameron & Associates)

"So many writers think picture books need to rhyme. There are some editors who won't even look at books in rhyme and a lot more who are extremely wary of them, so it limits an agent on where [that type of book] can go and the likelihood of it selling. It's also particularly hard to execute perfectly. Aside from rhyming, I see way too many picture books about a family pet or bedtime."

—Kelly Sonnack (Andrea Brown Literary Agency)

CONCERNING WHAT IS TABOO IN YOUNG ADULT BOOKS

"I would say this: Nothing is taboo if it's done well. Each scene needs to matter in a novel. I've read a number of 'edgy' young adult books where writers seem to add scenes just for shock value and it doesn't work with the flow of the rest of the novel. 'Taboo' subjects need to have a purpose in the progression of the novel—and of course, need to be well written! If it does, then yes, I would say nothing is taboo. Taboo topics do, however, affect whether the school and library market will pick up the book—and this can have an effect on whether a publisher feels they can sell enough copies."

—Jessica Regel (Foundry Literary + Media)

CONCERNING THE DEFINITIONS OF HIGH FANTASY VS. URBAN FANTASY

"In high fantasy, an entire world is created; it doesn't take place in what we recognize as the world as we currently know it. It usually has magic or magical creatures of some sort, though there are some exceptions. Urban fantasy takes place in what is recognizably our world and has vampires, werewolves, zombies, ghosts, etc. The stories involve characters that are human, or were once human, but have evolved into something else."

—Tamar Rydzinski (Laura Dail Literary Agency)

ON THE CONFUSION BETWEEN URBAN FANTASY AND PARANORMAL ROMANCE

"Urban fantasy vs. paranormal romance is always a fine line. I think urban fantasy lingers a tad longer on the wider plot, and paranormal romance lingers a tad longer on the chemistry between the two main characters."

—Robin Rue (Writers House)

"There is a lot of overlap in these two genres, but at its core, paranormal romance cannot exist without a romance. Urban fantasy can."

—Sarah LaPolla (Bradford Literary Agency)

ON MYSTERY VS. THRILLER

"The way I see it, a pure mystery is where the crime has already happened and the protagonist must solve it. In a thriller, the protagonist is often waiting for the crime to occur or working to prevent it. Mysteries can be more introspective, with a focus on the protagonist's mental powers of deduction, where thrillers are known for more action and physicality. In mysteries, a key element of the plot is hidden from the reader, such as (most traditionally) who the villain is. In a thriller, you often know who the villain is fairly early on, and the plot is centered around a game of cat and mouse."

—Cameron McClure (Donald Maass Literary Agency)

ON WHAT CONSTITUTES CRIME FICTION

"I would say that crime fiction is less about the whodunit than about the protagonist's dilemma in a criminal milieu. The protagonist may not have all the information—so there is a mystery in that he is trying to find something out—but the story is really about how he solves his problems, which are often as much about his lifestyle as about the particular crime that spurs the plot. For instance, in Ray Banks's brilliant Saturday's Child, *Cal Innes is forced by a local mob boss to find a former employee and the money he stole, but in many ways the story is about Cal trying to find a place for himself and form an adult life within a socioeconomic stratum that offers very few options."*

—Stacia Decker (Donald Maass Literary Agency)

ON WHAT MAKES A GOOD HORROR STORY

"Good horror isn't just about scares. It's about dark emotions: where they come from and how you deal with them. It can be hopeful; we see the protagonist fighting against this hell and it reminds us to be strong. It should be provoking, not that it shocks but that it makes readers think. Horror is more versatile than people sometimes give it credit for."

—Sara D'Emic (formerly of Talcott Notch Literary Services)

ON DEFINING TRAVEL NARRATIVE NONFICTION

"Travel and adventure narrative nonfiction is the type of book that takes you away to another place. It is often a memoir but also can be a journalistic story of a particular event or even a collection of essays. The key here is that it tells an interesting and engaging story. It is also very important these days that the story is fresh and new—you'd be surprised at how many people have had the exact same experience with the rickshaw in Bangkok that you had. Some successful examples of this genre are Jon Krakauer's Into Thin Air, *Elizabeth Gilbert's* Eat, Pray, Love, *and most things by Paul Theroux and Bill Bryson."*

—Abigail Koons (The Park Literary Group)

ON THE CATEGORIES OF CHILDREN'S FICTION

"In a nutshell: Early Readers = Frog and Toad and Elephant and Piggie. Chapter books = Judy Moody and Ivy and Bean. Think of the stages of development in this order: picture books lead to early readers, which lead to chapter books, which lead to middle-grade [books], which lead to young adult [books]."

—Jen Rofé (Andrea Brown Literary Agency)

"Early readers are for young kids just beginning to learn to read and are more heavily illustrated. Their language is restricted to basic words and concepts that help kids ages four to six learn to read. An example would be The Berenstain Bears. Chapter books are for intermediate readers ages seven to ten. Chapter books are for kids that are not quite ready for Harry Potter, but The Very Hungry Caterpillar isn't going to hold their attention either. Chapter books have illustrations but are primarily about the prose, and they have a bit more narrative complexity. Early readers can be indistinguishable from picture books and often have color illustrations on every page, whereas chapter books usually (though there are plenty of exceptions) have only black-and-white line illustrations sporadically interspersed. Early readers aren't usually more than 1,000 words, whereas chapter books are usually over 10,000 words. Both types of books are targeted at the school and library markets, so there are a lot of considerations when it comes to the vocabulary you should use. I would recommend doing a lot of research before attempting to write either sort of book."

—Evan Gregory (Ethan Ellenberg Literary Agency)

"A middle-grade book is generally intended for eight-to-twelve-year-olds, and the protagonist should be in that age range as well. YA is geared toward ages thirteen and up, although sometimes a YA book is classified as younger or older YA. Obviously subject matter must be appropriate for the intended age group, but equally as important is the voice. Too often the voice strikes me as too old or too young for the character's age. If the pro-

tagonist is an eleven-year-old boy, then the reader must feel like an eleven-year-old boy is speaking to them. An authentic voice makes the reader want to accompany that boy on his journey, whatever it may be."

—Ann Behar (Scovil Galen Ghosh Literary Agency)

ON CLASSIFYING EROTICA, ROMANCE, EROTIC ROMANCE, AND WOMEN'S FICTION

"The book crosses the line into erotica when the sexual journey is more important than the romantic journey—and that is not a bad thing, just a different market."

—Michelle Johnson (Inklings Literary Agency)

"To me, erotic romance is primarily between a couple (or sometimes a threesome) that will have a happily ever after. At its heart, it's the story of people finding their soulmates and exploring the connection via sex. Straight-up erotica doesn't have to end in a committed coupling. The focus (to me, and I'm sure others' [tastes] will vary) is more on the voyage of self-discovery ... a character or characters learning what it is that makes him or her happy and comfortable and finding the courage to accept whatever might be revealed."

—Lucienne Diver (The Knight Agency)

"A contemporary romance's plot revolves around the love/ romantic element, whereas women's fiction tends to revolve around women's issues and the growth and empowerment of the female protagonist. Women's fiction can have romance, but it's not the driving force of the plot."

—Kathleen Ortiz (New Leaf Literary and Media)

"Women's fiction novels are not simply stories with female characters, but stories that tell us the female journey. Women's fiction is a way for women to learn and grow, and to relate to others what it is to be a woman. When I think of literary fiction, on the other hand, the emphasis is placed more on the telling of a good story instead of making the female journey the centerpiece."

—Scott Eagan (Greyhaus Literary Agency)

ON MEMOIR CRAFT AND CONVENTIONS

"One of the worst things I see with memoir is when the writer starts from the beginning of their life to where they are now. Memoir should be only [cover an interesting period] of your life. I have been pitched memoirs that could be divided into three books! For memoir writers, choose your strongest or favorite theme and then work from exactly when it started to exactly when it ended. Do not include the before and after. I do not want to be reading a book from when you were two years old up until you are forty-three. It just doesn't work."

—Katie Shea Boutillier (Donald Maass Literary Agency)

"It seems like a lot of people miss the fact that the best memoirs explore universal themes. Readers need to be able to identify with what they're reading at least a little bit. Self-absorption, navel-gazing, axe-grinding, resentment—these things do not belong in memoir."

—Ryan Fischer-Harbage (The Fischer-Harbage Agency)

"I think everyone has a story to tell, and I understand how important and cathartic it is for people to tell their personal stories. That said, not all personal stories are ready for traditional publishers as developed. Of the memoir submissions that have come across my desk, I usually find they lack story arc or are autobiographies rather than memoir. Memoir is usually focused on a shorter period of time in one's life and is themed. If you want to pitch memoir, research genre guidelines (including word count) and be sure you have a strong story arc in place. Can you express what themes *your memoir is exploring? Is it a memoir of survival or loss? Do we see you change over the course of the memoir?"*

—Elizabeth Kracht (Kimberley Cameron & Associates)

"First and foremost, you've got to have an interesting story. Everyone thinks that their own life story is interesting, but it rarely is. Second, even though it's your story, there must be something about your story to which we can all relate. Third, your memoir should have a theme—it shouldn't just be a series of stories, but it should give readers the lessons you learned along the way. Most important: You shouldn't be afraid to put it all out there. If you're not going to be vulnerable and reveal your innermost fears and feelings and challenges honestly, then it won't resonate with readers. Truly great memoirs can be life changing for those who read them, and that should be your ultimate goal: How can I share my experiences with readers so that they can learn from them without having had to live through them?"

—Jennifer De Chiara (Jennifer De Chiara Literary)

ON WRITING AN LGBTQ NOVEL OR MEMOIR

"It drives me crazy that I get so many queer memoirs and coming-of-age novels where the author assumes that it's enough to just be gay and nothing much else is going on in their stories other than this identity crisis. I don't mean to trivialize that experience, but at the same time, many coming-out stories don't make for a riveting read or can sustain the scope of a novel on their own. This only works if you're writing at the level of someone like David Sedaris or Alison Smith."

—Cameron McClure (Donald Maass Literary Agency)

"If the protagonist's sexuality isn't an issue in the storyline—if the protagonist just happens to be gay—I don't think that book would be pigeonholed [as LGBTQ fiction]. But if the book is about the protagonist's gay lifestyle, then it would be categorized as such."

—Jennifer De Chiara (Jennifer De Chiara Literary)

ON THE CROSS-GENRE OF LITERARY HORROR

"Usually when I think of literary horror, I think of writers like H.P. Lovecraft, Edgar Allan Poe, and Shirley Jackson. Style-wise, I think what makes literary horror its own genre is the same as what makes literary fiction different from commercial fiction— heightened language, themes, concepts, etc. Only with horror, you get all the dark and gruesome elements, too. Added fun."

—Sarah LaPolla (Bradford Literary Agency)

ON WHAT MAKES A STORY A FIT FOR GRAPHIC NOVELS

"I'm looking for works that cry out to be told in an illustrative medium. It shouldn't be a book that you decided to draw because you thought it would look cool but a story with elements you felt you could only get across visually. And though it is visual, you still need all the elements you would have in a novel—a well-told story, narrative arc, character development, etc.—you can just find different ways to express them with your artwork."

—Jason Yarn (Jason Yarn Literary Agency)

ON DEFINING WOMEN'S FICTION

"For me, this comes down to novels about women by women. It's thoughtful, well-written, compelling novels about women's lives."

—Bridget Smith (Dunham Literary)

ON ANY CATEGORY OF BOOK THAT COMES WITH ILLUSTRATIONS (SUCH AS GRAPHIC NOVELS OR PICTURE BOOKS)

"I can't say this enough: If you're not a professional illustrator, don't have a friend/son/neighbor/grandchild illustrate your work. First, you want an agent to connect with your work on its writing merit (and not to dismiss it because he dislikes the art). Secondly, for picture books, it is almost always the publisher who makes the pairing between author and illustrator."

—Kelly Sonnack (Andrea Brown Literary Agency)

FURTHER RESOURCES

While I tried to cover everything in the world of agents throughout this book, space limitations meant that there was plenty left unsaid. The following is a list of resources that can help you along your way.

But while we're on the subject of learning more, let me say something about the duty of educating yourself about the craft and business of publishing. Continuing to educate yourself (even after you find some success) is important—*real* important. So learn, learn, and then learn some more. Take writing classes. Join a writing group. Read editor and agent blogs. Read novels to reverse-engineer and deconstruct why they worked so well. Attend writers conferences. Critique the manuscripts of others to become a better editor for your own work. Study books on writing. Do whatever it takes to constantly better your craft and knowledge.

But while you're out there soaking in information—especially when perusing the Internet—it's important to seek out a variety of sources to verify information. In other words, don't believe everything you hear. The fact is that 90 percent of what you read on popular blogs run by agents, editors, and writers will be good principles and worthwhile instruction. But the remaining 10 percent, in my opinion, more accurately reflects the quirk or opinion of a specific writing individual.

I've seen a writer trash-talk an agent online when the agent really did nothing wrong, and the writer was just posting sour grapes for all to see. If you believe what the writer says, you're needlessly dismissing a potential advocate for your book. I've seen an agent teach a writing class where she said, "You must end a query letter by revealing the ending of the book." In fact, revealing the ending of a book is a big query letter no-no, and it turns out the instruction was based on the simple fact that this particular agent liked to know how a book ends. If you took her personal preference as absolute truth, you'd be turning in a faulty query letter to many agents. I've seen an author personally tell an audience of writers how "a novel synopsis is a thousand words." But the gold standard for a synopsis is one page, single-spaced, making it about 500 words.

The point is: Not all the information on the Internet is true, and not everything you read or hear should be taken as gospel. Just because one industry professional says something doesn't mean it's an absolute truth, but if multiple sources are saying the same thing independent of one another, you're likely reading good advice. Educate yourself.

Self-Editing, Craft, and Plot

Revision and Self-Editing for Publication, Second Edition by James Scott Bell (Writer's Digest Books, 2012)

Plot and Structure: Techniques and Exercises for Crafting a Plot That Grips Readers from Start to Finish by James Scott Bell (Writer's Digest Books, 2004)

Save the Cat by Blake Snyder (Michael Wiese Productions, 2005)

The Plot Whisperer: Secrets of Story Structure Anyone Can Master by Martha Alderson (Adams Media, 2011)

Nonfiction and Platform

How to Write a Nonfiction Book Proposal, 4th Edition by Michael Larsen (Writer's Digest Books, 2011)

Create Your Writer Platform by Chuck Sambuchino (Writer's Digest Books, 2012)

Platform: Get Noticed in a Noisy World by Michael Hyatt (Thomas Nelson, 2012)

Bulletproof Book Proposals by Pam Brodowsky and Eric Neuhaus (Writer's Digest Books, 2006)

Book Proposals That Sell by Terry Whalin (Write Now Publications, 2005)

Twitter: @PlatformPundit, @JaneFriedman

Starting Strong/First Chapters

The First 50 Pages by Jeff Gerke (Writer's Digest Books, 2011)

Hooked by Les Edgerton (Writer's Digest Books, 2007)

Query Letters and Synopses

Formatting & Submitting Your Manuscript, 3rd Edition (Writer's Digest Books, 2009)

The Writer's Digest Guide to Query Letters by Wendy Burt-Thomas (Writer's Digest Books, 2009)

Blog: www.queryshark.com

Literary Agent Databases

Guide to Literary Agents by Chuck Sambuchino (Writer's Digest Books; always seek out the most recent, updated edition)

Blog: www.guidetoliteraryagents.com/blog

Database: www.querytracker.com

Subscription website: Publishersmarketplace.com, which is in tandem with the magazine *Publishers Weekly*, something else you should be reading

THE AAR CANON OF ETHICS

Note: This chapter is published with the permission of the Association of Authors'
Representatives. What you read below is their official Canon of Ethics as of 2014—
meaning that all full members of the organization must abide by these guidelines.

The members of the Association of Authors' Representatives, Inc. are committed to the highest standard of conduct in the performance of their professional activities. While affirming the necessity and desirability of maintaining their full individuality and freedom of action, the members pledge themselves to loyal service to their clients' business and artistic needs, and will allow no conflicts of interest that would interfere with such service. They pledge their support to the Association itself and to the principles of honorable coexistence, directness, and honesty in their relationships with their co-members. They undertake never to mislead, deceive, dupe, defraud, or victimize their clients, other members of the Association, the general public, or any person with whom they do business as a member of the Association.

Members shall take responsible measures to protect the security and integrity of clients' funds. Members must maintain separate bank accounts for money due their clients so that there is no commingling of clients' and members' funds.

Members shall deposit funds received on behalf of clients promptly upon receipt, and shall make payment of domestic earnings due clients promptly, but in no event later than ten business days after clearance; provided however that if funds for a client are received more frequently than quarterly and if those funds do not exceed a total of $100, then payments to clients may be made quarterly, so long as when funds received exceed $100 or upon the client's specific request, payment to the client shall be made within ten days thereafter.

Revenues from foreign rights over $50 shall be paid to clients within ten business days after clearance. Sums under $50 shall be paid within a reasonable time of clearance. However, on stock and similar rights, statements of royalties and payments shall be made not later than the month following the member's receipt, each statement and payment to cover all royalties received to the 25th day of the previous calendar month. Payments for amateur rights shall be made not less frequently than every six months.

A member's books of account must be open to the client at all times with respect to transactions concerning the client.

If a member receives in writing a claim to funds otherwise due to a client, the member shall immediately so advise the client in writing. If the member determines that the claim is serious, and that the funds should not be remitted to the client because of the claim, the member shall proceed in accordance with the following:

For a period not to exceed ninety days, the member may deposit the funds in question into a segregated interest-bearing account pending possible resolution of the dispute. No later than the expiration of that ninety-day period, if the dispute remains unresolved and the claimants do not otherwise agree with respect to the disposition of the disputed funds, the member shall take such steps as may be necessary to deposit the funds with a court of competent jurisdiction, with appropriate notice to the claimants, so that the claimants will have an opportunity to present to that court their claims to the funds. Upon so depositing the funds, the member will have complied with the member's obligations under this Canon of Ethics.

In addition to the compensation for agency services that is agreed upon between a member and a client, a member may, subject to the approval of the client, pass along charges incurred by the member on the client's behalf, such as copyright fees, manuscript retyping, photocopies, copies of books for use in the sale of other rights, long distance calls, special messenger fees, etc. Such charges shall be made only if the client has agreed to reimburse such expenses.

A member shall keep each client apprised of matters entrusted to the member and shall promptly furnish such information as the client may reasonably request.

Members shall not represent both buyer and seller in the same transaction. Except as provided in the next sentence, a member who represents a client in the grant of rights in any property owned or controlled by the client may not accept any compensation or other payment from the acquirer of such rights, including but not limited to so-called "packaging fees," it being understood that the member's compensation, if any, shall be derived solely from the client.

Notwithstanding the foregoing, a member may accept (or participate in) a so-called "packaging fee" paid by an acquirer of television rights to a property owned or controlled by a client if the member:

- fully discloses to the client at the earliest practical time the possibility that the member may be offered such a "packaging fee" which the member may choose to accept;
- delivers to the clients at such time a copy of the Association's statement regarding packaging and packaging fees; and
- offers the client at such time the opportunity to arrange for other representation in the transaction.

In no event shall the member accept (or participate in) both a packaging fee and compensation from the client with respect to the transaction. For transactions subject to Writers Guild of America (WGA) jurisdiction, the regulations of the WGA shall take precedence over the requirements of this paragraph.

Members may not receive a secret profit in connection with any transaction involving a client. If such profit is received, the member must promptly pay over the entire amount to the client. Members may not solicit or accept any payment or other thing of value in connection with their referral of any author to any third party for any purpose, provided that the foregoing does not apply to arrangements made with a third party in connection with the disposition of rights in the work of a client of the member.

Members shall treat their clients' financial affairs as private and confidential, except for information customarily disclosed to interested parties as part of the process of placing rights, as required by law, or, if agreed with the client, for other purposes.

The AAR believes that the practice of literary agents charging clients or potential clients for reading and evaluating literary works (including outlines, proposals, and partial or complete manuscripts) is subject to serious abuse that reflects adversely on our profession. For that reason, members may not charge clients or potential clients for reading and evaluating literary works and may not benefit, directly or indirectly, from the charging for such services by any other person or entity. The term "charge" in the previous sentence includes any request for payment other than to cover the actual cost of returning materials.

Notwithstanding the foregoing, members who participate in conferences or other events where writers are charged separately for individual consultations with agents in which the writer's work is read or evaluated may provide such consultations. The AAR believes that the potential for abuse presented by the practice of charging reading fees in such circumstances is mitigated by the fact that the agent is acting within the context of an independent writers' conference. Moreover, the concern that such participation would reflect adversely on our profession is outweighed by the potential benefit of such participation to writers, a benefit that cannot be duplicated in another manner.

It shall not be a violation of this paragraph 8 if a member provides an evaluation of a non-client's material if a) any payment therefor is made directly to a charity qualified under Section 501(c) (3) of the Internal Revenue Code or to an established educational institution; b) the member shall personally create the evaluation and provide it within a reasonable time; c) the member does not in any way benefit financially from the activity; and d) the member conducts the activity in an honorable way fully consistent with the AAR Canon of Ethics.

The provisions of the previous two paragraphs of this Paragraph 8 do not in any way dilute the AAR's belief that literary agents should not charge clients and potential clients for reading and evaluating literary works in the ordinary course of business.

INDEX

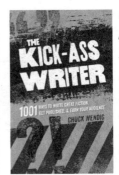